ONESHOT. **ONE**LIFE.®

proverbs 3:5-6

ONESHOT.
ONELIFE.®

The Ultimate Success Formula to
Help You Win At Anything in Life

DOUG FITZGERALD

NEW YORK

LONDON • NASHVILLE • MELBOURNE • VANCOUVER

ONESHOT. ONELIFE.®
The Ultimate Success Formula to Help You Win At Anything in Life

Published in New York, New York, by Morgan James Publishing. Morgan James is a trademark of Morgan James, LLC. www.MorganJamesPublishing.com

The Morgan James Speakers Group can bring authors to your live event. For more information or to book an event visit The Morgan James Speakers Group at www.TheMorganJamesSpeakersGroup.com.

Scripture quotations are taken from the Holy Bible, New Living Translation, copyright ©1996, 2004, 2007, 2013, 2015 by Tyndale House Foundation. Used by permission of Tyndale House Publishers, Inc., Carol Stream, Illinois 60188. All rights reserved.

ISBN 978-1-68350-865-6 paperback
ISBN 978-1-68350-866-3 eBook
Library of Congress Control Number: 2017918382

Cover Design by:
Christopher Kirk
www.GFSstudio.com

Author Photographs by
Jennifer Schultz

In an effort to support local communities, raise awareness and funds, Morgan James Publishing donates a percentage of all book sales for the life of each book to Habitat for Humanity Peninsula and Greater Williamsburg.

Get involved today! Visit
www.MorganJamesBuilds.com

Dedication

To Tammie, I could not do this life without you, nor would I ever want to. You are a blessing from God that I cherish. Thank you for your unwavering love, encouragement, and support. You inspire me every day as I watch you continually grow into the woman God designed you to be. It's beauty at its finest. With you I am complete!

To Dylan and Sydney, I am so thankful for each of you. It has been an absolute joy having a front row seat watching you fully live out your passions and dreams. You both inspire me! And every day I look forward to seeing how God is unfolding His plan for your future. Never ever let go of the dreams He has placed in your heart. Trust Him to direct your steps and never forget that He delights in every detail of your life.

You three have all my love!

Contents

Acknowledgments

There are so many people that I want to acknowledge and thank who have had a direct or indirect influence in the culmination of this book. I am truly grateful for each of you. Your friendship, encouragement, and love mean the world to me. Thank you!

God, my author
Roger and Kitty Fitzgerald, my parents
Mysi Girdlestone, my executive assistant
Joy Groblebe, my business coach
Cheri Gregory, my editor
Karen Anderson, my acquisitions editor
Sissi Haner, my proof editor
The Entire Morgan James Team, my publisher
Bryan Olesen, my inspiration brother
John Wooten, my creative & design guru
Traci Morrow, my btbtfw success partner

Introduction

The Wake-up Call

It happened on a perfect summer night around 2:00 am.

One of those rare times in our city, when you could look up into the night sky and see every star piercing through the dull haze of the city lights.

But the atmosphere was far from perfect inside our home.

You see, for a couple of years the relationship between my wife, Tammie, and me had become strained, to say the least. Each day it seemed to be getting worse, not better. The sarcasm, eye rolls, and sighs of disgust aimed at each other had spiraled out of control. It had gotten to the point where we had a hard time just being in the same room together. Our words were short, cold, and barbed. On top of all that, our pent-up frustrations and resentments toward each other consumed our thoughts nearly every minute of every day. And even when we weren't together, we still argued with each other in our minds, telling the other what we really wanted to say to set them straight.

That particular night, if you'd walked by our home and looked in, you would have witnessed the worst fight of our twenty-year marriage.

You know the kind: where you are trying to yell under your breath (so you don't wake up the kids) but every fifth word comes out loud, anyway. Where you simply want to scream at the top of your lungs, but manage, just barely, to hold it in.

So, at 2:00 a.m., I stormed out of the house.

I needed to take a walk to cool off.

If you had watched me go, you'd have thought I'd gone mad. All along the two-mile path that circles a seventy-acre park and high school football stadium, I was talking to myself, clenching my fists, yelling at my wife under my breath, and demanding to know why God put us in this situation. Every emotion inside was building up. I just wanted to scream and let out all of my pent-up rage.

About halfway down the path I got to a place where I felt I could let it all out and no one would hear me. With an empty football stadium on one side of me and no houses on the other, I raised my head and fists to the sky and yelled at the top of my lungs, "GOD, WHY ARE YOU DOING THIS TO ME?"

Instantly, I felt like I was standing alone on the fifty-yard line of the football field, hearing the *thump-thump* of stadium lights coming on like spotlights, and God's voice booming through the massive loud speakers.

"I'm not doing this to you," He said clearly and forcefully. "YOU are doing this to you!"

I felt like I had been punched in the stomach. My anger turned to an aching in my heart—a remorse that was literally gripping my soul deep inside me. My entire body trembled. Tears dripped off my cheeks. Mentally, emotionally, physically and spiritually, I was shaken to the core.

At that moment, I came face-to-face with the truth: I was putting my own needs first. I was ignoring Tammie's needs. I was the one causing the pain in our relationship. And I was the one who needed to initiate the healing.

This was the wake-up call that would radically transform our lives.

Chapter One

The Ultimate Success Formula Roadmap

"God, why are you doing this to me?"

Have you asked this question at some point in your life? Maybe for you, it sounded more like, "Why is this happening to me?"

Perhaps you asked it when a relationship was falling apart or slipping away.

Or when the bills kept piling up and you didn't know how you were going to pay them all.

Or when you got overlooked for a job promotion, laid off, or fired.

Or when you felt all your hopes and dreams were passing you by.

Or even when life seemed so overwhelming and meaningless that you considered throwing in the towel.

Life is not easy! Sometimes we get so overwhelmed that we seriously wonder why we were put on this earth in the first place. But there is hope—hope for a truly fulfilling life that will allow you to live out your life's purpose with great success.

It's been over six years since my 2:00 a.m. wake-up call from God. Tammie and I recognized that we'd drifted away from the biblical principles of success that we'd used early on in our marriage. So we began intently re-applying these principles and repairing our relationship.

The principles that helped us rebuild our marriage are the same proven principles that have been around for thousands of years. When we actively apply them, they bring success in every area of our lives, over and over.

I have personally used these principles to:

- Get out of tens of thousands of dollars of debt.
- Grow a savings and investment portfolio to take care of my family's needs.
- Develop a deep and loving relationship with my kids.
- Build a highly successful business and career.
- Lose over thirty-five pounds and maintain a healthy lifestyle for over fifteen years.
- Run two full marathons.
- Experience a growing faith in God.
- And so much more . . .

They can do the same for you.

For over twenty years, I have taught these principles to my family, friends, and thousands of people around the country with amazing results, and I can't wait to share them with you. I call this *The Ultimate Success Formula*.

In this book, I'll show you how to use five powerful principles to help you win at anything in life by:

1. Establishing clear priorities in each vital area of your life: Money, People (Relationships), Faith, Work, and Health.

2. Using a simple process to find a proven plan to help you achieve each of your priorities.
3. Applying critical secrets needed to master persistence in implementing your proven plans to completion.
4. Multiplying your success through effective evaluation.
5. Tapping into the life-changing power of having a success partner.

Whatever goals or dreams you have for your life, *The Ultimate Success Formula* is a proven roadmap to help you achieve them.

Here's how I'm going to help you implement *The Ultimate Success Formula* in the pages ahead:

- Each chapter covers one of the five principles.
- Throughout each chapter I give you ideas, tips, and exercises that relate to that chapter's principle.
- At the end of each chapter there are specific action steps to help you apply the ideas, tips, and exercises provided.
- You will then use *The Ultimate Success Formula Worksheets*, found in the back of the book, to complete each of the action steps.

Once you have completed every chapter, you will have a clear and detailed plan that will help you achieve success with each of your life's priorities.

Are you ready to get started?

Let's jump in!

Chapter Two

The Foundation Of
The Ultimate Success Formula

The Lord directs the steps of the godly.
He delights in every detail of their lives.
Though they stumble, they will never fall,
for the Lord holds them by the hand.
Psalm 37:23–24 NLT

We're about to dig into the five powerful principles of *The Ultimate Success Formula*—five biblical principles that have been proven to work for thousands of years. Principles established by God to benefit our lives and the lives of those around us.

Before we get started it's important to understand that God is for us! Period! He loves us and wants us to succeed at life. Too many times we allow ourselves to believe He is against us—just like I did that night when I yelled at Him.

By giving us these principles, God shows us that He cares intimately about the purpose and details of our lives. And not only does He care, He also promises to walk right beside us, helping us along the way.

This is why it's critical to understand the deep foundation that these five principles are based upon. A foundation that helps us determine our true intent for applying them in our lives. A foundation that can help us live a life of true contentment, satisfaction, fulfillment, purpose, joy, and happiness. A foundation that is the ultimate purpose of our lives.

This foundation is love.

Specifically, love for God and love for people.

When Jesus was asked about the most important commandment of God, he replied, "The most important commandment is this: 'Listen, O Israel! The Lord our God is the one and only Lord. And you must love the Lord your God with all your heart, all your soul, all your mind, and all your strength.' The second is equally important: 'Love your neighbor as yourself.' No other commandment is greater than these." (Mark 12:29–31 NLT)

In other words, all that we set out to do needs to be intentionally focused on growing deeper in love with God and each person who crosses our path. Focusing on this allows us to see how we can best impact the lives of others. That's why it's so vitally important to understand this foundation as you begin implementing these principles.

Thinking back to when Tammie and I were struggling in our marriage, deep down in our hearts we both wanted to have the best relationship possible. On the day we got married, we didn't look into each other's eyes and say, "I promise to be your enemy." We were best friends! We loved being together! We promised to stay together "'til death do us part"! Our focus was on making each other happy by meeting each other's needs; we each put the other first. Over time, however, we slowly began focusing on our own needs and stopped meeting each other's. This is when our relationship got way out of control, and we lost the joy and fulfillment of it in our lives.

I believe love is the most powerful force in the world because it can motivate us to do far more than we ever think is possible for others. True joy and fulfillment are found when we give of ourselves to benefit others. That's love. And I want to encourage you to remember this foundation as we dig into the five powerful principles of *The Ultimate Success Formula*.

TIP

Here's a tip to keep this foundation at the center of *The Ultimate Success Formula* process. Periodically stop and ask, "Is what I'm doing, or planning to do, allowing me to love God and others more?" This will keep your priorities grounded in the only thing that truly matters in life.

Chapter Three

Principle #1: Set Clear Priorities

Trust in the Lord with all your heart;
do not depend on your own understanding.
Seek his will in all you do,
and he will show you which path to take.
Proverbs 3:5–6 NLT

The first principle of *The Ultimate Success Formula* is this: **Set Clear Priorities**.

Priorities are the life choices you make that are crucial to your own success and the success of those whose lives you influence. Setting clearly defined priorities and taking regular steps to accomplish them allows you to take full advantage of every day of your life, giving you a true sense of purpose, accomplishment, and fulfillment.

Without clear priorities, it is easy to feel like your life is out of control, without purpose, in a rut, or—worst of all—that it really doesn't matter in the larger scheme of things.

That's why it's critical that we start with this principle first.

As we begin you might be thinking, "Oh, he's just talking about 'setting goals.'" But I want to widen your perspective by calling this process "*setting clear priorities.*" Here's why: the word *priority,* in and of itself, creates a sense of urgency. The definition of *priority* is "something that is more important than other things and that needs to be done or dealt with first."[1]

The Ultimate Success Formula is designed to help you achieve each priority that you identify as "vital" in your life. This will enable you to look back at the end of your life and say that you've done all you could to become the best you were designed to be. By doing so, you'll live a fulfilled life and leave behind a legacy that truly impacts the people in your world. A legacy where each person you touched will remember the difference you made in their life, whether big or small, and know that you truly cared about them.

The best thing you can do as you implement *The Ultimate Success Formula* is to ask God to help you discover your priorities and successfully live them out. Why? Because when we fully depend upon Him in all aspects of our lives, He promises to show us the direction to take and walk with us along the way. I have found that when I ask and trust God to lead me, He always does. Now, His leading doesn't always happen the way I envision or in my time frame. But, I always look back with a grateful heart, seeing that it was the best way. As you start this process, ask God to help you every step of the way.

---

1   Merriam-Webster, s.v. "priority," accessed December 11, 2017, https://www.merriam-webster.com/dictionary/priority.

Let's look at three critical areas that will help you set clear priorities. Once we have gone over these areas, I will give you specific action steps to follow that will guide you through to a final list of clear priorities for your life.

Identifying Your Priorities

I have found that one of the easiest places to get started to help you identify your priorities is to ask, "What am I currently worrying about?" The answer to this question will help you pinpoint some of your priority areas right away. I spent some time digging further into the area of worry to see how we can best use it to our advantage throughout *The Ultimate Success Formula* process.

CASE STORY: Worry

What Do You Worry About?

In the fall of 2016 I asked ninety-two people I know, trust, and admire—a pretty even mix of both men and women—this question:

> "*What do you worry about that often keeps you up at night (e.g., money, job, job security, relationships, health, faith, children, world issues)?*"

Initially, I didn't know what to expect, but I was deeply impacted by the responses. Nearly everyone gave thoughtful, honest, and in-depth answers.

As I complied and categorized all the answers, six primary concerns rose to the top: Money, People (Relationships), Faith, Work, Health, and Sex.

How about you? What do you worry about late at night? Which of these specific issues shared by these men and women can you relate to? Check any that apply to you.

Money
—— Having enough money to pay our bills each month.

—— We have so much debt that it's killing us.

—— Are we making wise financial decisions with our money?

—— Am I saving enough for retirement?

—— Will we be able to help pay for our kids' college education, wedding, etc.?

People
—— My wife and I are having problems with our marriage; I fear losing her.

—— Am I spending enough quality time with my kids? I want to be more involved with them and teach them how to make good choices.

—— I have no control over the life choices my kids are making (e.g., dating, driving, peer pressure, friend choices, social media, college decisions).

—— The physical safety of my wife and teens.

—— The effects of my divorce and all the insecurities that come with it.

Faith
—— Am I being the spiritual leader my family needs? I feel like I've been the "Spiritual Leader" in our home in name only, not by my actions.

—— The spiritual growth of my kids and their faith.

—— My personal faith. I feel stuck and really want to grow but don't know what to do. I feel lukewarm.

—— Discerning God's will for my life and my purpose as I make decisions that affect me and my family.

—— I don't really have a faith, but lately I've been asking myself "Is there a God?" And if so, I've been asking, "What am I missing?" and "What am I afraid of letting go of?"

Work

—— My job isn't fulfilling to me, but I don't know what to do.

—— I don't feel my job is secure; I could get laid off.

—— My job isn't bringing in the income that I really want and need.

—— I'd like to make a career change, but I don't know where to start.

—— I like my job but I am feeling overwhelmed and overworked. It's taking time away from me that I want to spend with my family.

Health

—— My physical health and the health of my spouse as we get older. We want to be physically active as we age.

—— I need to lose weight and live a healthier lifestyle to help with my diabetes, high blood pressure, and heart issues.

—— Being a good example to my kids. Am I teaching them enough about making good health decisions?

—— The declining health of my aging parents. Will I be able to fully help them like I want to?

—— The emotional health of my spouse and kids.

Sex

—— I want to be more sexually intimate with my spouse and have sex more often.

—— My body image holds me back sexually because I don't feel attractive.

—— Retaining my wife's physical attraction and desire for me.

—— There are issues in my past that are holding me back from being fully sexually intimate with my husband.

—— Whether or not my kids are having sex and how our culture is impacting how they view sex.

We all worry. Some of us more than others.

Worry is a broad human emotion with deep impact.

Worrying holds many people back from achieving the amazing things they were specifically designed to accomplish. Ultimately, it keeps them from becoming the person they desire to become.

Worrying can hold you back from achieving the big goals you have in your heart—the dreams you desperately want for your life and the lives of those around you.

Worrying can also destroy your health and cause you to make poor choices with negative results.

Worrying can cause you to:

- Feel exhausted
- Lose sleep
- Blow up at others
- Blow things out of proportion
- Lose your sex drive or hair or appetite
- Gain weight by stress eating
- Drink too much
- Feel sick to your stomach
- Become sick
- Suffer backaches

- Forget things
- Have panic attacks

And on and on and on.

Which of these effects of worrying have you experienced lately? (Trust me, when my wife and I were in the middle of our marital mess, we both experienced many of those effects.)

Worry

So, what is worry? In short, worry is feeling uneasy or concerned about something that's either currently happening or might happen to you or those you love. There are two main kinds of worry: worry over things you have control over and worry over things you don't have control over. And for most of us, WE WANT CONTROL!

Here's the great news: you can eliminate worry from your life and begin enjoying peace. It's not always easy, but you can start taking control of it rather than it taking control of you. If you want to start living worry-free, I have found that identifying the situations you *can* control is a great place to start as you begin to establish clear priorities for your life.

Are your finances in shambles? Is your marriage struggling? Does your job stink? Do you need to shed some pounds? Is your sex life unsatisfying?

You have the power to change each of these type of situations; as you do, you will worry less and begin enjoying peace more.

Worry You Can't Control

Of course, there are some things we do not have the power to change. A loved one might get in a car accident, get sick, make bad decisions, or treat you unfairly. When you worry about such things, they control you. Eliminating worry about things you can't control is difficult, but possible. Seeking help and support from God through prayer is a great place to start. In 1 Peter 5:7 NLT you are encouraged to "Give all your worries and cares to God, for he cares about you." In doing so He will give you the strength to turn your worry into a trusting hope and peace. Also, opening up and sharing with a good friend and/or a counselor can be a great help as well. **Just remember, what you can control is learning how to keep worry from controlling you.**

Three Critical Areas: Needs, Shoulds, and Wants

As you begin identifying your specific priorities, it is important to start by looking at these three critical areas of your life: Your Needs, Your Shoulds, and Your Wants. You will find most, if not all, of your priorities in these three areas.

1. Needs

Needs are things you have to take care of that are negatively impacting your life. As you just read, one great way to identify your true needs is by looking at what you worry about. Specifically, those things you know you have control over but haven't taken the necessary steps to control. Much of your worry is due to your inaction. If you want to eliminate your worry over things you can control, then you need to identify this as a priority, put together a plan to take care of it, and implement the plan. Doing this will help you stop worrying and start winning!

Ask yourself these questions to help you identify your Needs:

- What do I worry about that I *can* control? (Refer back to the Case Story about Worry and review the issues that applied to you, plus take note of any other issues not on the list.)
- What is a pressing issue in my life that will hurt me and those around me if I don't take care of it soon?
- Is there anything that I am holding back from doing that, if I did, would help me take an area of my life to the next level (i.e., something you're not doing because someone said you couldn't or that you weren't good enough or that you're afraid of)?

2. Shoulds

Shoulds are things you know are really important to do, but since you haven't placed any urgency on them, it's easy to put them off. The longer you wait to make them a priority, the more negative the impact will be on you and those you care about. We humans are really good at putting things off until the last minute but, ultimately, we know we will pay a price for our inaction one way or another. And if we wait too long, some of our Shoulds will eventually turn into our Needs.

I can't tell you how many times, during conversations about priorities, someone says, "You know, I really should do that." And that's when I say, "Don't *should* on yourself! Don't look back on your life and say, 'I *should* have done this or I *should* have done that.' Go do it!"

For example, many parents want to save money to help pay for their kid's college education someday. Say your daughter or son is two years old. The practical part of your mind says, "*If I simply save little by little over a long period of time, I'll be able to have enough to make a difference when the time comes."* But the impulsive part of your mind says, *"I'll never be able to save all that I'll need to, so why worry about it now. Plus, I've got more important things to spend my money on right now. I'll worry about it later."* For the next sixteen years you'll worry bit by bit and every time you think about it you'll tell yourself, *"I really should do that."* Then, when your child is a senior in high school, you'll regret that you failed to start saving back when they were two years old.

It is important to note here that there may be some overlap between your Needs and your Shoulds. And you may have identified some of your Shoulds as you read through the Case Story about "Worry." Keep this in mind as you begin identifying the Shoulds in your life.

Ask yourself these questions to help you identify your Shoulds:

- What things make me think to myself, *"I really should _____?"*
- Looking into the next five, ten, fifteen years or so, what things would I like to achieve that are important to me? What things will require consistency over a long period of time to achieve?
- If I were to die tomorrow, what are the most important things I should do today?

3. Wants

Too often, we ignore our heart's desires—desires that give birth to dreams deep within us. But sometimes we allow our dreams to be held captive inside our hearts, trapped by our own negative thoughts of them being irrational, unattainable, or irresponsible. Worse yet, we may even allow the negative thoughts, words, and actions of others to lock our dreams up deep within us. But I urge you, don't ignore your heart. Listen to it closely. Begin exploring it; give life to what it's telling you to pursue. Now is the time to get serious and start living the life you were born to live with the passions, gifts, and talents you were given. Don't hold back! You are given only one shot at this one life. So give it all you've got.

One of my favorite verses in the Bible is Psalm 37:4–5 NLT. It says, "Take delight in the Lord, and he will give you your heart's desires. Commit everything you do to the Lord. Trust him, and he will help you." God wants you to succeed in your Wants, so much so that He promises to help you achieve them. As long as your desires align with His overall plan and purpose for your life, He will be with you every step of the way.

Sometimes people tell me that they feel guilty or selfish for wanting to pursue their heart's desires. It's critical to understand that those desires, many of which God has purposely placed on your heart, are there for a reason. If your Wants align with God's plan for your life, you will find that they will ultimately serve and bless other people. I encourage you to fully pursue your Wants with passion. If you don't, who will?

Ask yourself these questions to help you identify your Wants:

- If I could do anything in the world, and money and time were not issues, what would I do?
- What did I used to dream about doing that I have since forgotten or intentionally buried?
- What did I dream about doing or becoming when I was a kid that I still think about today?
- What have others told me that I do well or that I should consider doing?
- What dream has God put into my heart?

Identify Your *Why*

Once you have identified your priorities, it's time to set yourself up for success. One key strategy I have seen drastically increase the likelihood of achieving one's priorities is identifying a strong emotional attachment—what I like to call a *Why*—to each of them. This strong emotional attachment will provide you the internal motivation to do whatever it takes to achieve your priorities.

A clear *Why* will also help keep your priorities in focus and in order. Often, when you sense that your life is out of balance and your priorities are out of whack, it can be traced back to not being clear or focused on your *Why*. That's why having a clear *Why* and understanding its purpose is so important.

Sometimes our *Why* is buried so deep within us that it's hard to get to and difficult to express clearly. We know it's there, but we can't see it. But unless you truly know what is at its core, you lose the power that it holds to help you do whatever it takes to achieve your priority.

In helping people identify their *Why*, I love to take them through a powerful exercise using a simple question that allows them to pull back the layers of their desire until they get to the core purpose of why they want to achieve a specific priority. Not surprisingly, that question is, "Why?" Once they answer, I continue to ask "Why?" until we get to the core of their *Why.*

CASE STORY: **Why**

The "*Why*" Exercise

A few years ago, I worked with a young man I'll call Bob. Bob had a dream to establish a successful health and fitness company in his hometown. He was frustrated because he didn't know if he could do it. He allowed his fear and self-doubt to hold him back from what he felt he was called to do. So, I started the "*Why*" exercise and our conversation went something like this:

Me: "Bob, why do you want to start this business?"

Bob: "Well, for a few years I've felt this overwhelming desire in my heart to do it."

Me: "Why do you have this desire?"

Bob: "Because I want to help people in my town with their health and fitness."

Me: "Why do you want to help them?"

Bob: *(Thinks for a minute. His voice cracks, and tears well up in his eyes.)* "I have watched several family members and friends suffer, and a couple even die, because of health-related issues. I know that if they'd had someone to help them take the initial steps to improve their health, they would not have had to suffer."

Me*: (Realizing that Bob is beginning to understand more deeply why he has this desire.)* "So why you?"

Bob: "I have the expertise and training to serve them and so many others in the town that I have grown up in and love."

Me: "Now we're getting somewhere. Give me some names that you are thinking of right now who you know could use your help. Tell me a little about their story and why they mean so much to you."

Bob: *(Lists names one by one and shares little bits of their stories. This goes on for half an hour.)*

Me: "So now do you think you can start to build this business?"

Bob: "Yes."

Me: *(For the last time)* "Why?"

Bob: "Because it hurts me to see my family, friends, and others in the community that I deeply care about suffer from health issues that I know I can help them with. If I can make a positive—and potentially lifesaving—difference in their lives, then that's what I want to do."

It's been several years since that conversation and Bob now runs his own successful health and fitness company that is truly fulfilling his *Why*.

Identifying and knowing your *Why* is built on the foundation of loving God and loving people. You see, when you pinpoint the *Why* of your priority, you'll find that at its core it involves your desire to live out your love for God by loving people. Whether directly or indirectly, your *Why* will be tied to people.

Now there might be times when you feel strongly about setting out to achieve a specific priority and may not totally understand how your *Why* will be carried out. That's okay—none of us can foretell the future. The key is having the attitude and anticipation of being a blessing to God and people.

For example, my son is a gifted baseball player. He absolutely loves it and is good at it. It's been his dream for years to play in college—which he is now doing—and in the pros, someday. Playing baseball is one of his priorities. His *Why* is to bring glory to God through the way he plays each game and encourages his coaches, teammates, and opponents. Since he has this attitude, he seeks ways to impact the lives of those around him while being the best steward of the gift and opportunities God has given him. (And the scholarship he earns sure doesn't hurt his parents any, either!)

Speaking of his parents, after our big 2:00 a.m. fight, Tammie and I had a long talk the next morning. We knew we needed to begin healing our marriage immediately or else we would risk losing it. Neither of us wanted that to happen. We talked about the dreams we'd had when we first got married and what we wanted our marriage to look like in the future. We re-visited our *Why* during our conversation. Our *Why* was and is: To have a marriage where we enjoy being together, grow deeper in love every day, encourage each other to live out the plan God has

Dylan Fitzgerald

for our lives, set a powerful example for our kids of how a healthy and successful marriage functions, and honor God at all times. Re-focusing on our *Why* motivated us to take the steps needed to work hard on our marriage. Our *Why* continues to give us the courage to make choices that lead to success.

Ultimately, your life revolves around your choices. No matter how big or small they are, your choices determine your future outcomes. And, every choice you make will also impact someone around you. That's why it's so important to establish clear priorities that will help guide you to make the choices that will lead to your desired success.

Now it's time to put this first principle of *The Ultimate Success Formula* into action. The time and effort you put into this first step will set the stage for some amazing success in your life that will not only impact you, but those around you as well. This is your moment to design your future, rather than having your future design you. So I urge you: Commit now to seeing this process through to the end. You'll be glad that you did!

Action Steps for

Principle #1: Set Clear Priorities

___ ***Action Step #1***

You will find *The Ultimate Success Formula Worksheets* for all of the Action Steps in the back of this book. You can either fill them out in the book or make copies of them and put them into a binder or folder to keep them organized and easily accessible. **A FREE digital download of the worksheets is also available at OneShotOneLife.com/Worksheets.** To complete the Action Steps, you will need:

- Worksheets
- Binder or folder (if you make copies of the worksheets)
- Pencil/pen
- Highlighter

___ ***Action Step #2***

Schedule time alone to sit down and go through *The Ultimate Success Formula* process. Make sure you have uninterrupted time that's free from distractions. This kind of environment can help you truly evaluate your life in a proactive and effective way. Also, don't feel like you have to do it all in one sitting. Feel free to break the process into a few sessions if need be.

TIP

If you are married, this is also a great exercise to do together as a couple. I suggest going through this process separately first and then coming back together once you have each identified your individual top priorities and sharing them with each other. You may find that in some areas you are both focused on the same priorities, and you can help each other in achieving them. You may also find that your spouse has some priorities that you don't or vice versa that might be worth considering aligning together. Either way, this is a great opportunity to intimately know each other's priorities and cheer each other on to success.

___*Action Step #3*

Pray and ask God to walk with you throughout *The Ultimate Success Formula* process. Prayer is a powerful way to have a two-way conversation with God. Share all that's in your heart with Him: your Needs, your Shoulds, and your Wants. Nothing is ever too bad or too good to talk with Him about. And then be willing to listen to Him. Sometimes you'll sense a prompting, hear His voice, be impacted by an experience, recall something you have read, remember a conversation with someone, or even hear nothing at all. Simply be open to Him leading you to the priorities that will fulfill His plan for your life.

___ *Action Step #4*

Go to the six worksheets titled "**Identifying My Priorities**." Each sheet has an area listed at the top: *Money, People, Faith, Work, Health, and Other*. We have identified these as the areas where most people find their priorities. For priorities that don't necessarily fit in the first five, use the "Other" worksheet.

For each of these areas, write down all of the priorities (Needs/Shoulds/Wants) you can think of that you would like to achieve. And I mean everything that comes to mind. Don't hold back. Nothing is too small or big to write down. If you run out of space on the worksheet, make more copies and keep on writing.

___ *Action Step #5*

In order to effectively achieve your priorities, it's important to first narrow them down by identifying your top priorities and then begin achieving them one by one so you don't get overwhelmed.

Go to each priority area sheet and, in the box next to each priority, put the number you feel best identifies its importance to achieve in your life (the legend for each number is at the bottom of each page). You will put a "1" next to those priorities you feel are VITAL to achieve, a "2" by those you feel are IMPORTANT to achieve, and a "3" by those you CAN WAIT to achieve. You can have as many of each number as you feel appropriately identifies each priority.

___ *Action Step #6*

Now that you have completed Step #5, it's time to prioritize your priorities! Your goal is to identify your top two in each area. Again, go to each priority area sheet and use a highlighter to begin crossing off the priorities you feel are not the most important for you to pursue to achieve at this specific time in your life. Start by eliminating those that

CAN WAIT, move on to the IMPORTANT priorities, and then finish with the VITAL priorities. Continue until you have identified your top two priorities in that area.

You may find that you only have one or even no priorities in some of the areas. That's okay. There may be certain times in your life when this may be the case. As long as you have purposefully and intentionally given your attention to each priority area, you are on the right track. Keep moving forward with the priorities you have identified.

TIP

Use a highlighter to cross off your priorities because you will want to continue to refer back to every priority you have written down over time. Don't delete any priority from your sheet or mind. Simply use Step #6 to identify your current top two priorities. As you begin achieving your priorities, you'll want to come back to your full list of priorities to find your next ones to pursue. Priority setting is an ongoing, ever-changing, and lifelong process for those who want to continually achieve great things with their lives.

___ *Action Step #7*

Now go to the worksheets titled "**My Top Priorities**" and write in your top two priorities for all six areas.

___ *Action Step #8*

Finally, with each priority, take time to really think about your *Why*. If necessary, use **The "*Why*" Exercise** found in this chapter to pinpoint your *Why*. Then write in your *Why* on the worksheet.

TIP

Make copies of the "**My Top Priorities**" worksheets that you filled out to place around the house or at work (e.g., on the fridge, bathroom mirror, by your desk, on your car dashboard, miniaturized to place in your wallet) for motivation.

CONGRATULATIONS! You are now a part of a very small and elite group of people who have intentionally identified the top priorities in every area of your lives.

Now it's time for you to take the next critical step toward achieving your priorities.

Chapter Four

Principle #2: Find A Proven Plan

Commit your actions to the Lord,
and your plans will succeed.
Proverbs 16:3 NLT

Plans succeed through good counsel . . .
Proverbs 20:18 NLT

N ow that you know your top priorities, you're ready for the second principle of *The Ultimate Success Formula*: **Find A Proven Plan**.

Benjamin Franklin said, "If you fail to plan, you are planning to fail!" You can have the greatest priorities mapped out for your life, but if you don't find a plan to use to achieve them, then you will be like the 42.4% of Americans who make New Year's resolutions every year and never achieve them, or, like the other 48.4% who have infrequent success.[2] Finding a plan is a key principle to achieving success with this formula.

And you don't want to find just any plan; you want to find a *proven* plan—one that has helped other people get the exact results you are looking to achieve. Don't try to re-invent the wheel or go it alone; there are plenty of proven plans available that provide many benefits.

6 Key Benefits of Choosing a Proven Plan

1. A proven plan will help you accurately assess your current situation so you know exactly where you are starting in the process.
2. A proven plan will provide a detailed roadmap with clear directions to follow to get you to where you want to go.
3. A proven plan will lay out specific action steps for you to follow to accomplish your priority.
4. A proven plan will set a realistic time frame for accomplishing your priority.
5. A proven plan will give you peace of mind as you take your first steps toward achieving your priority.
6. A proven plan will cost less time, money, frustration, and failure than if you were to come up with your own plan.

After Tammie and I decided to begin healing our marriage, she wanted to find a counselor right away, but I was reluctant. I was adamant that we figure out how to mend our relationship on our own, so I layered on the excuses. For starters, I had been a pastor for thirteen years and had helped counsel many marriages: "Why in the world would we need a counselor when I could do the counseling myself?" Plus, there was our

---

2   "New Years Resolution Statistics." StatisticBrain.com. https://www.statisticbrain.com/new-years-resolution-statistics/ (accessed December 11, 2017).

personal privacy to protect since I already knew some of the counselors in our relatively small city and didn't want them to know about our personal issues. And how could I trust them to counsel us the way I thought best? One by one I kept the objections coming. But finally, after Tammie's subtle encouragement, a close family friend's wisdom and prodding, and God's leading, we researched and found a counselor who walked us through a proven plan he and his wife had gone through successfully and that he had been leading couples through for decades. To this day, we are still using the tools, techniques, and wisdom of his counseling in our marriage.

Finding a proven plan can be one of the most difficult things you do when setting out to achieve your priorities. You may ask yourself: Where do I start? How do I find the best plan for me? There are so many options, how do I choose? Will the plan I choose actually work? This process can be very overwhelming!

Let me give you six tips to help you find a proven plan that will work. Tips I have discovered that will save you time, money, effort, frustration, and failure. Tips that will lead you to success.

Tip #1 to Finding a Proven Plan

Seek God's guidance and wisdom to help you find the best plan. God is so much bigger than our Needs, Shoulds, and Wants. He intricately planned, measured, created, and named the billions of stars in the universe. He created the world we live in and keeps it leaning at just the right angle, spinning at just the right speed, and traveling through space at 67,000 miles per hour around the sun so we won't burn up (or freeze) and die. If He can do all of that, I believe He can help each one of us find the right plan to help us achieve our unique priorities. He promises to. So start by simply asking Him to walk with you throughout this entire process.

Tip #2 to Finding a Proven Plan

Seek guidance and wisdom from people you trust. Sharing your priority and asking them for their input is a great way to find not just any plan but a plan that's been proven to work, either in their own lives or in the lives of people they know. Talk to family members, friends, business associates, experts in the field, pastors, and referrals.

Also, think of someone specific who has been successful in the priority area you are wanting to achieve. Ask if you can set up a time to talk to them about how they achieved their success. Offer to buy them lunch or take them out for coffee. Or maybe set up a phone call, video conference, or an in-person meeting. You'll be surprised at how willing people are to share what they know with you.

One group of people that our society has lost sight of, who can be our absolute best resource for guidance and wisdom, are those in the Baby Boomer generation and older. These men and women have incredible life experiences to offer, but, unfortunately, our culture tends to de-value their input and influence once they retire. Many feel the passions, talents, experiences, and skills they have acquired over their lifetime go dormant once they retire, but that is not the case. Sometimes the greatest honor we can give this generation is to ask them to share their guidance and wisdom with us. This is a great opportunity to allow them to speak into our lives. In my experience, every time I have asked for their insight, they are honored and thrilled to share. I highly recommend you make it a point to seek out someone in this phase of life who can give you their perspective as you search for your proven plan.

CASE STORY: Business Mentor

Back in 2013, I found myself at a frustrating point in my business. Our overall growth and income had plateaued. I was intently searching for the best plan to help propel it to the next level. Earlier that year, I was fortunate to meet a man who had run a very successful business of his own that he'd recently sold. From the moment we met, our personalities clicked. I asked him a lot of questions to learn about his business and how he had become so successful. He was excited to share the wisdom he had gained over the years, through success and failure. I asked him if he would be willing to give me his input on a small project I was working on. He agreed, and so began a mentoring friendship that I cherish to this day. Over the years, we have emailed each other, talked on the phone, and met in person. One of the most meaningful times we had together was when I traveled to his home halfway across the country. He had prepared two full days of one-on-one training to teach me the core principles of how he grew and developed his multimillion-dollar business.

From his mentoring, I learned and implemented several principles that have taken my business to the next levels of growth in organizational leadership, sales, income, and overall success.

I am continually grateful for the impact he has had in my life and for the friendship we have developed. And it all started by simply asking for his input.

I have found that the more you reach out to others to learn about their life experiences, the more opportunities you will have to find guidance and wisdom from those who cross your path. Don't be afraid to ask questions. Sometimes the biggest compliment you can give others is an opportunity to share about themselves. In doing so, you may find someone who is willing to help you in finding a proven plan. This can end up being the ultimate win-win situation for each of you.

Tip #3 to Finding a Proven Plan

Look into your past. Are there any plans you have used before that were helpful and effective? Is it possible you have drifted away from applying the steps that may have gotten you the results you desire today? Maybe it's time to pull them out of your file cabinet, tote box, or closet, dust them off and review them.

It might have been a book, video or audio series, seminar, online course, or a class that you found productive in helping achieve your priorities. It's definitely worth your time to jog your memory and see what you might find.

Back when Tammie and I were searching for a counselor, we remembered going to an eight-week, small group course, early on in our relationship, that was focused on building a strong marriage. Our curriculum was a book that we would read through together, discuss with our group, and then apply its specific plan to our marriage. It had a profound impact on our relationship.

When we began looking for a plan to heal and grow our marriage, we remembered how effective that course was for us, so we searched through our library, found the book, and committed to read through it again together. The interesting part is while we were going through the book, we decided to see if the author had a website with other resources or tools. It was there we found out that the author's son was a marriage counselor. Since we knew that the principles taught in the book were effective and what we desperately needed, we immediately contacted him and began our counseling. It was the best decision we could have made at the time, and it all came about by looking at what we had already experienced in our past.

See if there are any plans you have used in the past that you can re-apply today.

Tip #4 to Finding a Proven Plan

Choose a format that will motivate you to start, use, and track your plan. For example, say you find a great book that spells out a proven plan to help you clean up your finances by teaching you how to budget your money and get out of debt. If you love to read, learn best from books, and are likely to follow an author's plan, then this is a great format for you. But if you know you'll buy a book only to leave it sitting on your desk, untouched for months, then maybe an e-book, audiobook, video series, webinar, podcast, blog, computer program, mobile app, website, or membership site will work better for you.

Or perhaps you need personal interaction to get started and stay motivated. If so, then live seminars, conferences, small accountability groups, mastermind groups, classes through a church or organization or business, courses at your local college, one-on-one coaching, or counseling are formats you should consider.

Bottom line: proven plans come in many formats or combinations of formats. The key is to intentionally search for the one(s) that will motivate you to start, keep you engaged, help you track your progress, and give you the best chance for success.

Tip #5 to Finding a Proven Plan

Search the Internet and your local bookstore. If you are having a difficult time finding a plan or are just getting started, then some time on the Internet and/or a trip to an actual bookstore are in order.

While these are two very different places to find a proven plan, they each provide their own important benefits.

The Internet provides easy, private access at any time of the day from anywhere. That's why it can be a great place to start your search and give you a distraction-free environment. It is also a powerful tool that can provide you with access to plans for your specific priorities in a matter of seconds. Googling keywords and phrases that relate to your priority is a great way to get started. You can find experts, support groups, resources, local locations, and so much more.

WARNING

Let me give you a word of caution. While the Internet is a great place to search for your proven plan, anyone can start a website and call themselves an "expert." So be careful.

Here are a few ideas to help you find credible information on the Internet:

1. Start with sites you already know and trust.
2. Ask your friends for suggestions of places you can search.
3. Make sure the site and content is up to date and relevant.
4. Read the bios and credentials of the people providing the information on the site.
5. Do a search of trusted reviews for the content you are considering.
6. Look for a few options before choosing your final plan.

On the other hand, sometimes you may need an actual "experience" that gives you a hands-on opportunity to explore for your proven plan. A local bookstore can give you that "experience." It also gives you the ability to interact with store employees who can help guide you. If you are unsure of what to look for or where to look, ask an employee. They can be a great resource in helping you find exactly what you are looking for.

One of my favorite places to go for inspiration and information is my local Barnes & Noble bookstore. There's something powerful about physically searching for information. It engages your senses. The feel of the books, the smell of the store (and a new book), and the hunt for a plan can make it a fun and exciting experience. Give it a shot.

While your personality may easily lend itself to one or the other, consider both as options.

Tip #6 to Finding a Proven Plan

Check in regularly with us at OneShotOneLife.com where we are continually developing and growing a carefully curated list of proven plans. You will find effective resources and tools that will help you achieve your priorities in the areas of Money, People, Faith, Work, Health, and Sex. Some of the resources include our weekly Ultimate Success Formula Email, The **ONE**SHOT. **ONE**LIFE. Show (OSOL Show), YouTube and Facebook videos, the online video course, blog posts, seminars, live events, mastermind groups, one-on-one coaching, free downloads, and more.

You can find all of this information, as well as links to our social media accounts, on our website at OneShotOneLife.com.

Now that we've looked at the benefits of a proven plan and reviewed some tips to find one, it's time to put this second principle of *The Ultimate Success Formula* into action.

When completing the first principle, you established the clear priorities you want to achieve. Now it's time for you to find the proven plan that will lead to success with your established priorities.

Principle #2: Find A Proven Plan

___ ***Action Step #1***

Do a quick review of your "**My Top Priorities**" worksheets. You will use these worksheets in the next step.

___ ***Action Step #2***

Now find the worksheets titled "**My Top Priority Plan**". Each worksheet has one of our identified areas listed at the top: *Money, People, Faith, Work, Health, and Other.*

Starting with your top priority in the area of *Money*, find the corresponding "**My Top Priority Plan**" worksheet that has *Money* listed at the top of the page. Fill in one of your priorities along with your *Why*.

Note: If you have more than one top priority listed in an area that you want to begin pursuing, you will need to make more copies of that specific "**My Top Priority Plan**" worksheet. A FREE digital download of the worksheets is available at **OneShotOneLife.com/Worksheets**.

___ *Action Step #3*

Use the six tips that we covered in this chapter to find a proven plan for your priority. Once you have your proven plan, write it down on the sheet.

___ *Action Step #4*

Repeat Action Steps #2 and #3 until you have gone through all of your priority areas listed on your **"My Top Priorities"** worksheet.

Note: Leave the rest of the blanks on the "**My Top Priority Plan**" worksheet empty. You will fill them in after we go through the third principle of *The Ultimate Success Formula.*

WAY TO GO! You have now completed all of the steps in the first two principles of *The Ultimate Success Formula!* Now it's time to move on to the third principle and put your plans into action.

Chapter Five

Principle #3: Master Persistence

Good planning and hard work lead to prosperity,
but hasty shortcuts lead to poverty.
Proverbs 21:5 NLT

Finishing is better than starting.
Patience is better than pride.
Ecclesiastes 7:8 NLT

You've identified your top priorities and found proven plans to help you achieve them. Now you're ready for the third principle of *The Ultimate Success Formula*: Master Persistence.

Persistence is the one key principle that will lead you to succeed. It's easy to set your priorities and find proven plans to achieve them, but where most people fail is in carrying out the day-to-day activities of each plan so they can experience its benefits. They fail at persistence.

How many times have you set up a diet plan, only to quit after a few days? Purchased a workout program or gym membership, only to feel guilty for not using it? Bought a book to help with finances (or relationships or career) only to let it collect dust on a shelf? Signed up for an online course to help you achieve your dream of creating extra income, only to forget the login and password after a couple of weeks?

We've all established a priority, found a plan to achieve it, and then dropped the ball shortly after getting started—if we got started at all. Clearly, persistence in carrying out the plan is absolutely critical for us to experience success with our priorities.

Persistence is the one thing that clearly separates the successful from the wannabes. Persistent people continue implementing their plan despite any difficulties, frustrations, and setbacks they may experience. The truth is, most people want what successful people have, but they are not willing to do what successful people do to get it: persist.

Are you willing to do whatever it takes to achieve your priorities? Since you have made it this far into *The Ultimate Success Formula* process, you have already demonstrated a rare level of persistence. Way to go and keep up the great work! Now it's time to step it up even more and commit to this final principle.

CASE STORY: Best Advice

Some of the best advice about persistence I've ever received came from an absolute stranger. Six months after Tammie and I launched a new business, we went to Las Vegas for a corporate event. That weekend, we went out to dinner at an Italian restaurant in the Wynn Hotel to celebrate our anniversary. Luke, our waiter, was an elderly gentleman who had moved to the United States from China to earn money to take care of his family back home. Since the restaurant wasn't busy that night,

Luke chatted with us quite a bit. We explained to him that we were in town for a new business we had started and that I was getting ready to resign from thirteen years as a pastor to build this business full-time. Luke could tell we were nervous and excited.

"You will be very successful with the business," he told us. "But I have one piece of advice that will be a key to your success."

He got a blank receipt from the wait station, brought it back to our table, and wrote his name on it in English and Chinese. Then he drew a Chinese symbol called Ren and added the word "Endurance."

Ren Receipt

"The symbol represents a knife over a heart. Any time you set out to do something you are passionate about and you know is important, the process will not always be easy to achieve. You will have great days and difficult days, but if you keep heart and endure through the process over time with a high level of discipline, consistency, and growth, you will enjoy the benefits of success."

My wife and I both felt that Luke's message was an answer to prayer, assuring us that starting our business was what we were to pursue.

It's been over ten years since that night Luke shared his wisdom about endurance with us. Wisdom that has proven itself true over and over again. There have been many days where we have wanted to throw in the towel and quit because of the struggles and emotions that building a business can bring: frustration with people, lack of confidence, pain of failure, fear of the future, and so on. But because we continued to focus on our passion and endure through these difficulties, there have been even more days where we have celebrated the growth of our business and the benefits it has given to our family: financial security, peace of heart and mind, a sense of purpose, control over our time, the ability to achieve growth without limits, and more.

As you begin implementing your priorities, know that the process won't always be easy. You will have good days and bad days. Life will get in the way. Distractions and difficulties will come. You may even question if your priorities are worth pursuing and consider throwing in the towel and quitting. But I encourage you to be persistent in implementing your plans, because in doing so you will experience the incredible benefits that achieving your priorities will provide.

I've paraphrased a Chinese saying that reminds me to endure and persist:

The rich with endurance will protect their home.
The poor with endurance will save themselves from humiliation.
The father and son who endure show affection and respect.
The siblings who endure show righteousness and sincerity.
The friends who endure make their relationship last.
The husband and wife who endure live in harmony.
In the middle of a difficulty, those who endure may be ridiculed by others.
But, once one overcomes the difficulty, those who ridiculed will be ashamed.

Let's look at three tips that can help you master persistence.

Tip #1: Be Disciplined

Unfortunately, most people consider discipline as something negative. They think discipline takes away fun and replaces it with boredom. Or that discipline is punishment for doing something wrong (which is also no fun). We forget discipline's ultimate purpose: to help you stay focused on specific steps that will get you the results you desire.

Ultimately, discipline is all about your mindset. As you look at the priority you want to achieve and the plan you have identified to make it happen, you must focus on doing each of the steps that lead to success. Make a decision now to be disciplined as you follow your plan.

In Mark Batterson's book, *Chase the Lion: If Your Dream Doesn't Scare You, It's Too Small*, he shares the inspiring story of how discipline was the key to George "Shotgun" Shuba's success.[3]

> George "Shotgun" Shuba went on to play seven seasons for the Brooklyn Dodgers and was on the 1955 World Series championship team.
>
> In his celebrated baseball book, *The Boys of Summer*, Roger Kahn said Shuba's swing was "as natural as a smile."[4] Shuba laughed at Kahn's description.
>
> During an interview with Kahn, Shuba walked over to a filing cabinet and pulled out a chart marked with lots of Xs. During the off-season, Shuba would swing a weighted bat six hundred times a day. And that was after working his off-season job all day! Every night he'd take sixty swings and then mark an X on his chart. After ten Xs, he'd give himself permission to go to bed. Shuba practiced that daily ritual for fifteen years!

3   Mark Batterson. *Chase the Lion: If Your Dream Doesn't Scare You, It's Too Small* (New York: Multnomah, 2016).

4   Roger Kahn. *The Boys of Summer* (New York: Harper Perennial; Reissue edition, 2006), 224.

"You call that natural?" Shuba asked Kahn. "I swung a 44-ounce bat 600 times a night, 4,200 times a week, 47,200 swings every winter."[5]

Just like George "Shotgun" Shuba, you can take specific actions to help you not only develop discipline, but stay disciplined as well. Let's look at five methods that can help you get a disciplined start to your plan.

Get a Disciplined Start

Here are five ways to help you get a disciplined start as you begin implementing your plan.

1. Set a start date and a completion date for your plan. Beginning is good, but finishing is always better. Setting start and completion dates will draw a line in the sand and move you down the road of discipline. Set your dates and get rolling.

LIFETIME PRIORITY

In some cases, you may find that the priority you want to accomplish is one you hope to live out for a lifetime, long after you've succeeded with your plan. For instance, if you have a plan to implement a family budget, the reality is that you will want to continue budgeting for the rest of your life. You will definitely have a completion date for the specific plan you are using. Once you have achieved the plan's initial desired outcome, continue carrying out your plan's specific

---

5   Kahn, *The Boys of Summer*, 241.

steps. In most cases, you will find that those steps will become a subconscious habit that you will want to evaluate periodically.

2. Post copies of your "My Top Priorities" list. Put them where you can see them throughout the day (e.g., bathroom mirror, office desk, refrigerator, car). You may also want to consider making it the background graphic on your computer or phone. And if there is one specific priority you are laser-focused on over the others, make copies of the "My Top Priority Plan" worksheet for that priority and post it as well. Doing this will provide a conscious, and subconscious, focus on your priorities, which will help keep you disciplined.

My son Dylan had a unique way of keeping one specific priority in front of him, so he would see it every day. After his freshman year in high school, it was his top priority to make the varsity baseball team as a sophomore. So, he pulled out a marker and wrote the word "VARSITY" in big, all capitalized letters on his dresser mirror to see it every day and be motivated to do whatever it took to make the team. He worked relentlessly in the off season to prepare for tryouts. Unfortunately, he didn't make the varsity team that year, but he did make the junior varsity squad.

Not making varsity was a letdown, to say the least, but he used that disappointment to motivate him even more throughout the year. So, he kept "VARSITY" on his mirror until the next season's tryouts. All of his continued hard work and training paid off when he made the varsity team as a junior.

If you walked into his bedroom today, you would still see "VARSITY" on his mirror. Why? Because it's still his top priority and it continues to motivate him. Not only did he make varsity his senior year in high school, he has made the varsity team as a freshman and sophomore in college as well. And I have a feeling "VARSITY" will remain on his mirror for a few more years to come.

So never underestimate the power of posting your priorities in prominent places to keep you motivated every day until you achieve them.

3. *Treat your plan like a job.* In order to succeed, you will need to focus on your plan intently, so treating it like your job can provide great discipline. With a job, you have to be on time, work when you're scheduled, do what is required of you, and excel at your position if you want to advance. If you don't fulfill those things, you will either be reprimanded or fired. Likewise, the level of effort you put into your plan will determine the level of your success. If you have a priority that you consider vital to your success, your family's success, and/or those around you, then treating your plan like a job by sticking to a set schedule, doing the work that is required, and giving your best effort can be a great way to stay disciplined in carrying it out to completion.

4. *Schedule specific days and times to work on your plan.* Consistency is critical. One of the top problems people have in implementing their plan is staying consistent. Many start, but within a few days or couple of weeks, they stop. To help you stay consistent, I highly recommend you set up a regular schedule and stick to it. A good way to start is to put your scheduled times on a calendar for the duration of the plan. Better yet, put them on your electronic calendar (computer or phone) and program it to remind you. Stick to your schedule, and over time you will see the results of your work.

5. *Use a tracking calendar.* Create and print off a calendar of your scheduled activities. As you complete them, put a check mark or "X" on the date to show your progress. You'll stay focused and feel a sense of accomplishment as you follow your plan.

Tip #2: Be Patient

Anything worthwhile in life takes time to achieve. It doesn't matter if you are practicing to become the best guitar player in your city, working toward the next job advancement in your company, saving to pay for your daughter's wedding, mending your relationship with family members, or exercising to lose fifty pounds.

It all takes time.

As a good friend of mine says about weight loss, "You didn't gain it overnight, so don't expect to lose it overnight." While you probably want the end result immediately, it is important to understand that it will take time and that there is value in embracing the process with patience. A plan that is worked over time will produce amazing benefits if you patiently see it through.

Some of the most valuable lessons you can learn in life, and some of the most treasured moments you will experience, will be found while implementing your priority's plan. But you will only see and treasure those things if you are intentionally looking for them as they happen. Learn how to patiently lean into the process.

Our daughter, Sydney, is an incredible dancer. Her dancing touches the hearts and emotions of the people who watch her, not to mention her mom and dad. But what most people don't see is the time she has put into practicing her technique, choreography, expression, storytelling, and so much more. She understands that in order to rise to the level she desires, she must put in the time working her plan, trusting that she will see the growth and the desired results months and years down the road.

Because of her incredible passion, discipline, and God-given ability, Sydney has always been placed in the higher-level classes, where she is usually several years younger than all the other dancers. This hasn't happened by accident or luck. Every year, she sets a priority of what class level she wants to achieve for the next year and asks her dance instructors specifically what she needs to do to get there. With achievement of the next class level as her motivation, she patiently puts in the time needed to develop the skills to get her to that next level. She has done this for years with success every time. And on top of that, she has experienced some incredible lessons and special moments along the way.

Embrace Patience

Here are four ways to help you embrace patience as you carry out your plan.

1. Continually envision the end result you desire. Sometimes we lose hope and quit because we lose sight of what we are trying to achieve. Finding ways to keep your end result in front of you on a regular basis can help you stay motivated and patient, knowing that in the end your effort will pay off. Using pictures, sayings, verses, mementos, songs, or anything else that reminds you of your end desire are great ways to achieve this.

For example, if you are restoring your marriage, surround yourself with pictures that remind you of what your relationship was like when you were both the happiest (e.g., dating, wedding day, with your kids). You can do the same with special sayings or verses, or you can listen to "your song" regularly. If you are working towards purchasing a home, have your family help you pick out a picture of the type of home you want and put it on your refrigerator. If you are losing weight, pull out a favorite dress or pair of jeans that you want to fit back into and hang it on your closet door. If you are growing your faith, find the Bible of a family member whose faith you deeply admired and keep it in the place where you regularly study and pray.

Be creative and have fun finding ways to keep your end result in front of you,

2. *Find role models who have achieved the end result you desire.* Look up to them as inspiration along the way. Read their success stories, watch their videos/movies/documentaries, and/or talk to them in person, if possible. Their testimonies will give you a patient hope to continue moving toward your priorities.

3. *Regularly journal about your experiences.* Throughout the process, remember and reflect on the lessons, achievements, and special moments you are given. Writing is a great way to process your feelings and document your progress. Journaling will help you keep a healthy and patient perspective while you are achieving your priorities. It's also a great tool to use to regularly look back to see how far you have come and enjoy the progress you have made.

4. *Recognize and reward your achievements along the way.* Often, we find ourselves impatient, wanting the end result "now"! We crave the satisfaction and reward of the achievement before we've actually earned it. A great way to curb your impatience is to taste little bits of your success throughout the process by purposefully recognizing and rewarding yourself—and anyone else who is directly impacted by the priority you are working towards. Find specific mile markers of achievement throughout your plan and establish how you will reward yourself for getting to each point. Then, once you achieve your mile marker goal, celebrate. My one caution: don't reward yourself with something that will be counterproductive to your plan or that might cause you to derail. Make your rewards positive, practical, and fun.

Tip #3: Be Growing

It is inevitable that throughout the process of carrying out your plan, you are going to go through a roller coaster ride of emotions and situations. If you have a setback or make a mistake, you may question whether it's worth it to continue. If you are not seeing the results right away, you may wonder if the plan is even going to work. If it takes longer than you are anticipating, you may throw in the towel and give up all together. On the other hand, if you have a great day or unexpected moment of success, you may get overconfident and wonder why you need to continue on with the plan since you've obviously "got it all figured out."

It's because of these emotional lows and highs that you need to anchor yourself to a solid commitment of working your plan all the way through. A powerful way to keep a steady emotional pace is to focus on your own personal growth.

Personal growth is simply the process of continually learning and developing skills in various areas of your life that will reveal a wealth of value in the future. And in order for personal growth to truly take hold, it must become a habit practiced over time. Committing to personal growth will cut through the clouds of self-doubt, setbacks, mistakes, discouragement, and even successes so you can see your plan through to the end.

When Tammie and I were going through the first several months of marriage counseling, our emotions constantly ran the gamut. One hour we'd feel great about our progress, and the next hour we'd be totally frustrated with each other. Or sometimes when one of us was feeling optimistic about our situation, the other seemed to be feeling bad. It was an emotional roller coaster of ups, downs, twists, and turns. But it was our commitment to personal growth that allowed us to persist through the initial phase of counseling long enough to begin experiencing meaningful change in our marriage.

During that time in our lives, Tammie focused on her daily times of Bible study and prayer. God led me to a video Bible study series by James MacDonald called "When Life Is Hard: Turning Your Trials into Gold." The encouragement and growth we experienced because of our personal growth enhanced the overall effect of our counseling by allowing us to stay grounded and focused until we started to experience some amazing success in our relationship.

This is one of many reasons why I believe personal growth is vital for everyone to pursue on a daily basis, no matter where you find yourself in life.

Develop Personal Growth

Here are three ways to help you develop personal growth as you work your plan.

1. Read, listen, or watch every day for personal growth. A great way to get started is to set aside time every day where you can read fifteen pages of a book, listen to fifteen minutes of an audio, or watch fifteen minutes of a video. Since everyone learns differently, I want to encourage you to use a medium you enjoy most and will keep you interested and motivated. Some people like to read, some like to listen, and some like to watch. Whichever works best for you, use it. And feel free to mix them up or use them together. A lot of times when I am reading a really good book, I'll also get the audio version and listen to it while I am riding in my truck or going for a jog around the neighborhood. Plus, it's a good idea to pick a time and place where you won't get distracted easily so you can soak in what you are learning.

2. Carve out time for personal growth. Over and over I hear people say that they just don't have time for personal growth. But there really are no excuses if you want to make this a regular part of your life. Here are just a few ideas to help you find that extra 15–30 minutes in your schedule:

- Wake up 15–30 minutes earlier in the morning when it's still quiet around the house.
- Make it part of your bedtime ritual 15–30 minutes before you go to bed.
- Go into work 15–30 minutes earlier before others show up.
- Use your daily drive time and carve out 15–30 minutes.
- Re-arrange your lunch time to squeeze in 15–30 minutes to feed your soul.
- If you work out, take 15–30 minutes to work out your mind at the same time.
- Do you regularly take your kids to activities or practices? If so, take 15–30 minutes while you wait.

3. Choose quality resources for personal growth. It's important, as you begin to carry out a personal growth plan, that you use quality resources and tools that meet your specific needs. Here are some ideas of where to get started:

- The Bible
- Biblically-focused books or studies
- Books that focus on the priority areas of your life
- Blogs
- Audio books
- Podcast series
- Videos
- Great quotes or scriptures to memorize

Ten Great Personal Growth Books/Audiobooks:
There are so many great personal growth books that have been written. Here are ten that have had a profound impact on my life and would be a great place to start if you are currently looking for one.

1. *The Bible*
2. *Gripped by the Greatness of God* by James MacDonald
3. *Chase the Lion* by Mark Batterson
4. *The Power of Positive Thinking* by Norman Vincent Peale
5. *The 15 Invaluable Laws of Growth* by John C. Maxwell
6. *The Strangest Secret* by Earl Nightingale
7. *The Blessing* by John Trent & Gary Smalley
8. *Fully Alive* by Ken Davis
9. *Rich Dad Poor Dad* by Robert T. Kiyosaki
10. *The Richest Man Who Ever Lived* by Steven K. Scott

Now that we've looked at three specific tips to help you implement your plan with persistence, it's time for you to put this third principle of *The Ultimate Success Formula* into action. In completing the first principle, you established the clear priorities that you want to achieve. The second principle helped you identify specific plans to help you achieve your priorities. This third set of action steps is designed to help you stay persistent in implementing your plans.

Action Steps for

Principle #3: Master Persistence

___ *Action Step #1*

On the "**My Top Priority Plan**" worksheets that you have begun filling out for each of your priorities, fill in the "Start Date" for your plan.

___ *Action Step #2*

Fill in the "Completion Date" for your plan. Keep in mind, this date may change as you begin implementing your plan. You may get ahead or behind schedule. Either way, it's okay. The overall goal is to complete your plan successfully no matter how long it takes.

___ *Action Step #3*

Next, fill in the "Weekly Schedule" for your plan. Here you will write down the day(s) and time(s) you have scheduled into your calendar when you will be implementing your plan.

___ *Action Step #4*

Finally, there were several other tips presented to you in this third principle. If you want to give yourself the best chance at successfully completing your plan, implement the tips that really spoke to you and that will provide motivation for you along the way. Please do not overlook them. If you need to, test them out to see which ones will work best for you. Go back now, review them, and write down which ones you want to use in the "To-Do/Notes" section on this worksheet.

CONGRATULATIONS & WAY TO GO! You are now part of the elite 3%. Author Brian Tracy says, "Only 3% of adults have clear, written, specific, measurable, time-bounded goals, and by every statistic, they accomplish ten times as much as people with no goals at all."[6] This is a tremendous accomplishment, and, you should be extremely proud.

Now you are ready to learn about two bonus principles that will propel your success to the next level and give you the absolute best results possible with *The Ultimate Success Formula.*

---

6   "Setting Goals and Objectives: 5 Myths." BrianTracy.com. https://www. briantracy.com/blog/general/setting-goals-and-objectives-5-myths/ (accessed December 11, 2017).

Chapter Six

The Multipliers:
Two Bonus Principles To Help You Multiply Your Success

Using a dull ax requires great strength,
so sharpen the blade.
That's the value of wisdom;
it helps you succeed.
Ecclesiastes 10:10 NLT

My child, don't lose sight of common sense and discernment.
Hang on to them, for they will refresh your soul.
They are like jewels on a necklace.
They keep you safe on your way, and your feet will not stumble.
You can go to bed without fear; you will lie down and sleep soundly.
Proverbs 3:21–24 NLT

H ave you ever said to yourself, "If only I'd known then what I know now, I'd have done some things differently"? I've said it to myself hundreds of times.

Like the time I took a stock tip from someone I didn't know and invested $1,500 into a company that was sure to double my money. Yep, a few weeks later the stock tanked, and I lost over $1,200.

Or the time when Tammie and I were dating but living in two different cities. We were so in love, and I wasn't monitoring the time we were spending talking on the phone—back when long-distance calls were billed by the minute. You can imagine my surprise when my first phone bill was over $500. Yeah, I threw up a little in my mouth after opening that bill.

And there was the time when my sister's car was leaking radiator fluid, and I tried to be a helpful big brother. Unfortunately, I unscrewed the radiator cap right after she'd driven an hour to my apartment. The cap shot off like a rocket and hit me in the face. Scalding hot fluid sprayed all over my right arm, landing me in the ER with severe burns.

Or how about the time when I ran into a high school friend I hadn't seen in a while at the Walmart photo counter. I asked, "So, when are you due?" only to have her respond, "I'm here to pick up pictures of the baby I had last week."

If only I'd known then what I know now, I'd have done some things differently!

Life is a great teacher. You can gain so much practical knowledge through the process of living. And if you are willing to learn from the past, you will benefit from it in the future.

Unfortunately, some people don't learn from their own mistakes. They turn their past failures into regret and guilt, wishing they had made different choices. Instead of learning, they either end up making the same mistakes over and over, or paralyze themselves from taking action to change their lives for the better.

But here's the great news: when you identify what you could have done differently through your past experiences and start making the appropriate changes, you begin developing life-changing wisdom.

Wisdom is simply taking your knowledge and experience, and often the knowledge and experience of others as well, and applying them with common sense and discernment to produce benefits for your life and the lives of those around you.

The Ultimate Success Formula is a culmination of the wisdom I have personally gained over the years through learning from my past experiences and many mistakes. Wisdom that's added real value to my life by producing positive results. And those experiences have helped me clearly understand and refine the principles that you are learning about in this book.

While implementing the principles of *The Ultimate Success Formula* over the past twenty years, I've discovered two powerful principles that, when applied, will help you achieve your priorities much faster and multiply your success many times over. I wish I had known about these two principles years before I discovered them because they would have motivated me to do some things differently, giving me far greater success in many areas of my life. I call these two principles **The Multipliers**.

The Multipliers helped me get out of debt years earlier than I expected, lose weight far faster than I anticipated, grow a couple of businesses larger than I dreamed, and heal my marriage far beyond what I ever hoped.

Make no mistake: **The Multipliers** do take extra work, more time, focused intentionality, and full initiation on your part to be effective while you are carrying out your priorities and proven plans. But they are worth it. They will give you back so much more than you invest into them. When you harness their power, you will reap benefits far beyond what you can imagine.

If you are looking to get the absolute best results out of *The Ultimate Success Formula*, implement **The Multipliers**.

Chapter Seven

Multiplier #1: The Extraordinary Benefits Of Evaluation

How wonderful to be wise,
to analyze and interpret things.
Wisdom lights up a person's face,
softening its harshness.
Ecclesiastes 8:1 NLT

The first Multiplier is to take advantage of **the extraordinary benefits of evaluation** by regularly evaluating your progress as you live out your priorities and proven plans. Stepping back to review your progress—or lack of progress—is a great way to help you stay focused.

Throughout *The Ultimate Success Formula* process, you may feel overwhelmed, stuck, or even lost—like you're not making any progress or have totally stopped implementing your proven plans altogether. Regular evaluation will provide you with valuable insights that will help you get re-calibrated, re-focused, re-aligned, and re-energized. As a result, you'll start seeing greater progress and success.

Tammie and I have an ongoing joke in our house. I love Tammie to death, but she does not have one technological bone in her body. (Correction: she did just let me know she's sure she has at least one little technological bone in her body.) It seems like whenever she touches anything electronic, something inevitably goes wrong. It doesn't matter if it's her cell phone, computer, printer, or TV; if it has electricity and a computer chip, it's at war with Tammie, and she is always on the losing end. Now I'm far from a being a tech guru, but I know enough to be dangerous, so I'm the go-to guy in our family to fix any tech-type problems.

At least once a week, Tammie asks me one of these questions:

- "My phone is acting weird, and I can't get it to work. Will you help me?"
- "I was working on my computer, and now it's locked up. Can you fix it?"
- "The printer's not printing. What do I do?"
- "The TV remote is not working. What's wrong?"

And my answers to all her questions are always the same three questions of my own:

- "Did you turn it off and then back on?"
- "Did you unplug it and plug it back in?"
- "Did you update the software?"

No matter how many times Tammie has the same exact problems, she still asks me the same exact questions, and I respond back with my same exact questions. And nine times out of ten, that fixes the problem.

Why do those three answers work most of the time?

1. Turning an electronic item off and back on allows it to do a basic reset of itself. This stops what was not working, so it can start back up again working correctly.
2. Unplugging and plugging back in an item usually allows it to do a more in-depth reboot. This forces it to re-calibrate its own software, clean out the problem, and start up again, almost as if it's brand new.
3. Updating an item's software allows it to be fixed from the outside. Those who created it are continually working to improve its performance and correct any problems that might crop up. They provide updates to make it the best it can be at any moment in time.

Regular evaluation of your proven plans can provide similar benefits and results.

The Benefits of Regular Evaluation of Your Proven Plans

First, regular evaluation can allow you to identify what's not working correctly and help you to easily get back on track to using your plan as it was intended to be used. Usually you'll find that along the way you have modified the plan a little, left out steps, lost focus, or lacked commitment to the time necessary to get the results you want. Regular evaluation can provide minor course corrections that will allow you to work your plan as intended.

Second, regular evaluation can provide a deeper look into why your plan is not working and offer a more in-depth personal alignment to your plan. In this case, you may find that you have not given your full attention to implementing it as needed, you have allowed other things in life to drown out your focus on it, you have taken the liberty of making major changes to it, or you have not bought into the plan itself believing that it will actually work. Regular evaluation can provide a major reset that will allow you to get re-focused and re-committed to the plan by cleaning out anything that is getting in the way of it working as intended.

And third, regular evaluation can provide any fixes and improvements to help you get greater results from your plan. If you are fully committed to implementing your plan and starting to see the success you desire, then you may identify and look for ways you can upgrade your plan, opening a new phase of learning and growth that will provide compounding results.

Years ago, I asked a highly successful friend, who was in his mid-fifties, what his secret was to achieving consistent success in his career over a long period of time. This top executive at a major U.S. company told me that every year he re-invents himself. He looks at what he's doing and evaluates whether it's effective and meeting his priorities. He then keeps what's working, throws out what's not, and searches for new ways to keep building and growing his business. He's constantly learning through the practice of regularly evaluating his plans.

The Benefits of Regular Evaluation of Your Priorities

Regular evaluation also has the same benefits when you apply it to your overall priorities as well. Scheduling time to regularly evaluate where you are with your life priorities is critical to staying on track and succeeding in the areas you have identified as the most important in your life.

Sometimes, you may feel like your life is out of control, and you don't know what to do. It is important to know that this is normal for most people to feel from time to time and that you are not alone! Many times, if you will step back and take some time to evaluate your priorities, you will find that you have either not given them the focus and attention needed, or you have placed other less important things in front of them. Then you can take the necessary steps to re-align and re-calibrate your priorities to get yourself back on track.

That feeling of being completely out of control with my life, and especially my marriage, was exactly what I was experiencing that night I yelled at God. All God did was tell me to step back and evaluate my life and marriage from a broader perspective. In doing so, I was able to clearly see that over time I had allowed my priorities to get way out of whack because I'd been neglecting the actions I knew I needed to take to build up my relationship with Tammie. Not only did this evaluation of our lives and our marriage allow us to re-align and re-calibrate them, it also helped us to see the vital need to implement regular evaluation into our relationship.

Specifically, we are applying regular evaluation to our marriage by having a date once a week. Every week we have a scheduled time when we intentionally spend time together, just the two of us. We may go to a movie, go shopping, run errands, or just hang out together. But we always eat lunch together, pray, talk about what's going on in each of our lives, discuss important decisions that need to be made, celebrate the wins, comfort each other through difficulties, and, ultimately, ask each other how we are doing in meeting each other's needs. We have done this for over five years now, and it's one of the highlights of our week.

TIP

If you are married, I highly recommend you start implementing a weekly date time into your schedule. Make it a priority. You may have a crazy busy schedule, you may be juggling young kids at home, you may have prioritized other people over your spouse, or you may have a list a mile long of other reasons why you feel you can't do this. But the truth is, you and your spouse can't afford not to do this. You need to find a way to implement a date time into your weekly schedule so you don't lose the most vital relationship in your life. This will take some effort and planning to implement. You may even

> need to get creative! Take a walk, go out for coffee, eat dinner, grab
> some ice cream . . . But please don't underestimate the power of
> spending intentional one-on-one time alone with your spouse to talk
> about life. It will pay huge dividends in your relationship.

Five Key Evaluation Questions

Here are five key questions to ask when evaluating your proven plans
and priorities.

1. What is currently working?
2. Can I improve upon what is working? (Only pursue that
   which will lead to greater success and productivity.)
3. What is currently not working?
4. Can I change or eliminate what is not working? (Only pursue
   that which will lead you to greater success and productivity.)
5. Is there anything new that I can learn about and implement?
   (Only pursue that which will lead to greater success and
   productivity.)

As you can see, regular evaluation can propel the success of your
priorities and plans to a whole new level by showing you how to be
more productive as you learn and grow from your experiences. I love
how pastor Andy Stanley puts it. "Experience alone does not make
people wiser. Evaluated experience makes us wiser."[7] When you put your
evaluated experience to work, you will experience greater success.

Now let's put this Multiplier to work by completing the following
action steps.

---

7   Czarina Ong, "Andy Stanley shares how people can start over successfully."
     Christian Today. https://www.christiantoday.com/article/andy-stanley-shares-how-
     people-can-start-over-successfully/54494.htm (accessed December 11, 2017).

Multiplier #1: The Extraordinary Benefits Of Evaluation

___ ***Action Step #1***

Go to the "**My Top Priority Plan**" worksheets that you have begun filling out for each of your priorities.

___ ***Action Step #2***

Choose a specific day of the week to regularly evaluate your proven plan and progress, then write it in the "Evaluation Dates/Times" space on your worksheet.

TIP

I recommend that you review your most critical plans daily. You may find that some plans only need to be evaluated on a weekly, biweekly, or monthly basis. I highly recommend that the time frame you choose be no longer than once a month. A good way to start implementing this is to schedule your evaluation time on your calendar. And better

---

yet, put them on your computer (or phone) calendar and program a reminder. You might also consider making your review a part of your routine after you wake up in the morning or before you go to bed at night. These actions will create a habit of regularly engaging with your plans.

___ *Action Step #3*
Now go to the worksheets titled "**My Top Priorities.**"

___ *Action Step #4*
Choose a specific day of the month to regularly evaluate your priorities and progress, then write it in the "Evaluation Dates/Times" space on your worksheet.

TIP

I have found through my own experience, and the experience of those I have worked with, that regularly evaluating your priorities every month is the most effective time frame to keep you focused and successful in achieving them. The longer you go without evaluating your priorities, the easier it is to neglect them and allow them to get out of whack. Also, as you start achieving your priorities, you can identify others to start actively working on.

Chapter Eight

Multiplier #2: The Remarkable Power Of A Success Partner

Two people are better off than one,
for they can help each other succeed.
If one person falls, the other can reach out and help.
Three are even better,
for a triple-braided cord is not easily broken.
Ecclesiastes 4:9–10,12 NLT

Walk with the wise and become wise . . .
Proverbs 13:20 NLT

The second Multiplier is to tap into **the remarkable power of a success partner** who will hold you accountable to your priorities and proven plans. Someone who will walk beside you step-by-step through your exciting journey and help you cross the finish line, while adding deep value to your life.

Making the bold and life-changing decision to establish clear priorities and set out to achieve them is no small task. You will experience many twists and turns along the way. Many people who try to do it all by themselves not only struggle alone, but oftentimes give up, leaving their hopes and dreams behind. We were not designed to live life alone. We were created to live life together so we can help each other succeed. That's why it's critical to surround yourself with people who will cheer you on to success every step of the way.

A painting on my office wall regularly reminds me of the deep value that success partners have added to my life. The painting is titled "Victory, O Lord!" by John Everett Millais[8], and it depicts a powerful scene in the Bible of two men, Aaron and Hur, intently holding up the arms of Moses who is too tired to do so on his own.

Here's why.

The nation of Israel, which was led by Moses, was being attacked by an enemy army—the Amalekites. Moses climbed to the top of a hill with Aaron and Hur so he could watch the battle and lead his army by holding up the staff that God had used to demonstrate His power and presence to the people of Israel. "As long as Moses held up the staff in his hand, the Israelites had the advantage. But whenever he dropped his hand, the Amalekites gained the advantage. Moses' arms soon became so tired he could no longer hold them up. So Aaron and Hur found a stone for him to sit on. Then they stood on each side of Moses, holding up his hands. So his hands held steady until sunset." (Exodus 17:11–12 NLT) As a result, Israel won the battle.

One of the key takeaways from this story is the incredible value of having committed partners supporting you as you set out to achieve your priorities. Moses had a plan to carry out; Aaron and Hur stayed right beside him to make sure he got it done! Period. Personally, I don't

---

8   John Everett Millais, "Victory, O Lord!" http://www.victorianweb.org/painting/
      millais/paintings/19.html.

even think Aaron and Hur even questioned whether or not to help Moses. I believe they knew Moses and his priorities so well that they probably ran ahead of him up the hill, found the best spot for him to stand (and eventually sit), and cheered him on throughout the battle. I can hear them saying, "Moses, you got this. Keep going. You're doing great! Don't give up. If you get tired, we'll hold up your arms. We got your back. We'll be here with you to the end."

And when the battle finally ended, I can guarantee you they yelled screams of victory so loud that everyone in the valley below and back at camp could hear them. Plus, you know they gave Moses hugs, high fives, and might have even carried him down the hill on their shoulders.

And to top it off, they were probably right by his side for hours after the battle, consoling and encouraging him as he had to lead his army and people through the pain and sadness of the lives lost on the battlefield that day.

Success partners are people like Aaron and Hur who commit to do what it takes to encourage you to succeed throughout the highs and lows of the process. For me, having a success partner has been the ultimate Multiplier in helping me squeeze out every ounce of success possible with my priorities and proven plans. I have seen this play out the same way in the lives of people who commit to this Multiplier, and I know you will experience the same as well.

But before we move on, please understand that a healthy and productive success partner relationship is a two-way street. The benefits you experience will also be the benefits your success partner will experience as well. The commitment is between both of you as you set out to support each other through the process. As much as Aaron and Hur encouraged and supported Moses, I'm sure that Moses encouraged and supported them in return.

Common Questions About Success Partnerships

In order to get the most benefits possible out of this Multiplier, you must intentionally develop and foster relationships with success partners. As I have worked with people who consider implementing this remarkably powerful principle, they seem to always have the same three questions:

1. "Why do I need a success partner?"
2. "How do I find a success partner?"
3. "Once I have a success partner, what do we do?"

Let me give you some insight and practical steps to apply as we answer each of these three questions.

"Why do I need a success partner?"

First, let's look at some of the benefits a success partner can provide. A success partner will:

- Provide accountability to help you achieve your priorities.
- Want the best for you at all times, rooting you on to success.
- Never make you feel like they are competing with you.
- Give you clear and honest feedback as you implement your plan.
- Identify if you are staying on course or not and keep you on track with your plan.
- Cheer you on to keep going when you feel like giving up.
- Listen to your thoughts/concerns/ideas/frustrations/struggles and act as a sounding board to help you process them.
- Share their feedback, suggestions, insight, and wisdom to help you be more effective and successful.
- Celebrate your successes with you.

- Allow you to share all of the above benefits with them as you help them to achieve their priorities as well.

I hope by now you can see the tremendous value a success partner can give you and why you should pursue adding this key Multiplier to *The Ultimate Success Formula* process. If you know deep down you could use any or all of those benefits, then you need a success partner.

Yesterday I received a text from one of my success partners that I have been meeting with for nearly ten years now that sums up the benefits very clearly: "I could have NEVER survived over the years without those many, many, many heart-to-hearts."

CASE STORY: A Challenge For Men

If you are a guy going through *The Ultimate Success Formula*, and you are like most men, you would probably rather go through the process alone for various reasons. One main reason is that we tend to find it hard to open up to others about the true condition of our lives. I've found that a lot of guys are crumbling under the pressure of so many things on the inside, but you would never know it on the outside because they put so much effort into hiding what they are actually going through.

While Tammie and I were going through our marriage counseling, our counselor encouraged me to do something he said was vital for the male friends in my life. He told me that once Tammie and I were in a healthy place in our relationship, he wanted me to share what we had gone through with my married buddies. So every time I had lunch or coffee with a friend, and he asked, "How have you been?" I would say, "I'm doing great now, but over the past couple of years Tammie and I have been really struggling with our relationship. We have been seeing a counselor for several months now, and I can honestly say that our relationship is better now than it has ever been."

Every guy I shared that with had nearly the same exact response, "You guys went through that? My wife and I are going through a rough time right now, and I thought I was all alone. We're at a point where I am wondering if we'll be able to make it through and don't know what to do."

These small moments of transparency have opened the door for other men to see that there is hope. Moments that started conversations where I could offer encouragement, point them in the direction for help in their marriage, and start regular meetings with some of them as success partners. We strengthened each other while striving to build the best marriages possible.

Guys, I challenge you to get outside of yourself and find a success partner. I truly believe you need a success partner to be the best you can possibly be in the priorities you have set out to achieve. I have benefited from having success partners in all areas of my life, and I know you will too.

"How do I find a success partner?"

Finding a success partner can be intimidating and challenging, especially if you have never had one before. It can be a difficult task if you don't know where to begin. You may even feel inadequate, intimidated, and embarrassed as you start this process, but don't let emotions get in your way. Your feelings are completely normal and will quickly turn into relief, excitement, and deep gratitude once you find and begin working with your success partner.

One powerful way to work through these initial feelings is to refer back to your "**My Top Priorities**" worksheets and read through your priorities and "*Whys*" again. Ask yourself, "Why are these my top priorities? What will I miss out on, and what will others around me miss out on, if I don't attack them with focused urgency?" Your answers to these questions will motivate you to move ahead with confidence and clarity.

When people begin this process, they often tell me, "I don't have time to find a success partner, let alone regularly meet with one!" But the truth is, you can't afford *not* to have a success partner if you are serious about achieving your priorities at the highest level of success.

Hearing someone say they don't have time for something of importance reminds me of my good friend Jeff, who cuts to the chase when people blame their lack of progress on their lack of time. "It's not that you don't have time," he always says. "It's that you choose not to make time for it."

We all choose how we spend our time. That's why it's vital to be intentional with it. If achieving your priorities is of utmost importance to you, then you must arrange your schedule and commitment to see it through. And the same goes if you choose to implement this Multiplier.

Five Steps to Finding a Success Partner

It is very important to understand that you will need to take the initiative to find a success partner. This process doesn't just magically happen. It takes time and effort. Let me give you five steps that I have found to be very effective in finding a great success partner.

Step One: Ask God to help you find the right success partner. I am continually amazed how God so often answers this prayer in my life and in the lives of those I see go through this process. He may help you identify someone you already know, cross paths with someone you haven't had contact with in a while, or meet someone new. And the fun part is when you begin sharing your thoughts of possibly teaming up with this person, they will have been on the same search but didn't know who to approach about it.

Step Two: Identify the specific priority and/or plan you want to work towards with a success partner. This will help you identify someone who wants to achieve the same results you do. They may be just starting out like you or have already achieved a certain level of success in that area; either way, they can make a great success partner.

Or maybe you are looking for a success partner who wants to focus on their overall life priorities like you are doing with *The Ultimate Success Formula*. This is a great way to help you stay focused on *The Ultimate Success Formula* process.

Be clear on what you want to achieve with your future success partner. This will help you identify a partner and clearly explain to them what you want to achieve when you ask them.

Step Three: Don't automatically default to the easiest ask. Too many people follow the path of least resistance and ask a good friend. Don't assume your best friend will make the best success partner. While they may be a great friend, they might not be a great fit. Evaluate your potential partner to make sure they are the best fit for you.

Here are some traits to look for in a great success partner:

- Similar priorities
- Reliability

- Good listening skills
- Candor
- Honesty
- Transparency
- Willingness to ask difficult questions
- Accepting of positive criticism
- Maintains confidentiality with your conversations
- Desires your success as much as their own

Keep in mind that you will need to have and/or develop these traits as well!

TIP

If you don't know your potential partner very well, I highly recommend you go over this list with them and let them know you are committed to living out these traits and would like to team up with someone who is committed to do the same. If you decide to become partners, establish a future date when you will evaluate your partnership to see if it's meeting both of your needs. Initially, I recommend doing this after the first three months. This will give each of you a chance to decide if this is working or not. If it is, you can continue on and re-evaluate every six months; if it's not, you can stop your partnership at that time.

Step Four: Brainstorm a list of people you might consider to be your success partner. Many people struggle with knowing where to look to find a success partner, but the truth is that there are people all around you who are potential partners and who would be honored to team up with you. The key is to be attentive as you start looking.

Write down the name of anyone who might meet the priority and/ or goal you are trying to achieve. Once you've built a list, you can start narrowing down and prioritizing who you want to ask to join you. Also consider asking someone you trust for any ideas of who might make a good success partner for you.

Success partners can be an individual or a group of people working to achieve the same priorities/plans. Don't limit your search to individuals alone. If you find that working with a small group of people might be a better fit for you, consider joining and/or starting your own mastermind group that is focused on specific priorities and/or plans.

Personally, I have developed several mastermind groups over the years where I have met with a group of people on a regular basis. My current mastermind group consists of me and two other guys. The purpose of our group is to focus on achieving success with our families and businesses, although we usually end up encouraging each other in various areas of our lives. We currently meet in person once a month at a local restaurant, and we commit to meeting together for a year at a time.

I also have an individual success partner that I have been meeting one-on-one with for nearly ten years. Our purpose is to focus on our overall life priorities and plans to make sure we are each being as effective as possible. We currently meet through a video conference once a week, and I don't see us stopping any time soon.

Over the years, I have focused on various priorities and plans, with different numbers of people, for various lengths of time, through changing seasons of my life and in many formats (in person, over the phone, and video conferencing). Keep your mind open and be creative as you work through this process.

Here are some ideas of places to look to help you identify a success partner:

- Your current circle of friends
- Co-workers
- Business organizations
- Church
- Community groups
- Social media acquaintances
- Health club
- Support groups
- People you respect and look up to
- Parents in your kid's school or activities

WARNING

If you are married (and even if you aren't married), please be very careful when considering a success partner of the opposite sex. Going down this path lends itself to some issues that can damage your relationship with your spouse if you are not careful.

Here are a few guidelines to follow when considering a success partner of the opposite sex:

1. Before making the decision to have a success partner of the opposite sex, talk it over with your spouse first to get their perspective, opinion, and consent. Honestly look at it from their point of view and make the decision together.
2. If you decide to work with a success partner of the opposite sex, establish the following parameters:
   a. Have your spouse meet your success partner before you start your regular meetings.
   b. Schedule all meetings in advance and make sure your spouse knows when they are scheduled.

    c. Never meet alone with your success partner when meeting in person. Meet in an open area visible to the public or bring someone with you, like your spouse or a trusted friend. Clear these types of meetings with your spouse.

    d. If you are doing regular meetings by video/computer/phone, make sure they are done in a room that is open to others, specifically your spouse. And always let your spouse know they are welcome to sit in at any time.

3. Regularly evaluate the purity, focus, and concerns regarding the relationship with your success partner with your spouse.

4. If your potential success partner is married, have them follow the same process.

Following these guidelines will not only protect the most valuable relationships in your life, but will ultimately enhance the success you achieve.

Step Five: Go for the ASK! Once you have identified the person or people you want to ask, then do it. This is your chance to step up to the plate and swing for the fences—a chance to become transparent and vulnerable by sharing your Needs, Shoulds, and Wants with someone in hopes that they are looking for something similar as well. Remind yourself that this is just as much an opportunity for them and their success as it is for you and yours. The fun part is that when you find the right person or people, they will be just as excited to get started as you are.

Here are six things to consider when asking someone to be your success partner:

1. Set up a time to meet with them when you can both be free from distractions and where you can have an in-depth, meaningful conversation.
2. Let them know there is absolutely no pressure for them to say "yes" to the idea you're going to share with them and that it's absolutely fine with you if they decide this is not for them.
3. Be clear on what you are specifically asking them to do before you actually ask them. Prepare to share specifics about your Needs, Shoulds, and Wants. Be ready to tell them that you are looking for someone to walk alongside you during this process. You may or may not have everything you are going to do figured out at this point, and that's okay. Simply share with them what you have at this point and ask if they'd consider joining you.
4. Give them time to ask questions, think about it, and decide if it's the right fit.
5. Give them a specific time frame to let you know whether or not they will decide to join you. Ask if you may contact them within the next week to see what they decide.
6. Finally, thank them for considering your proposal.

Review: The Five Steps for Finding Your Success Partner
1. Ask God to help you find the right success partner.
2. Identify the specific priority and/or plan you want to work towards with a success partner.
3. Don't automatically default to the easiest ask.
4. Brainstorm a list of people you might consider to be your success partner.
5. Go for the ASK!

I am confident that as you diligently follow these five steps you will find a success partner who will help you achieve your priorities and plans, and then take them to the next level of success!

"Once I have a success partner, what do we do?"

Once you've found a success partner, remember that the two of you are investing intentional time in helping each other advance forward with your priorities and plans. To avoid wasting time, you'll want a structured format for your meetings. Failure to plan means failure to grow.

My success partner meetings all share a common format. Regardless of whether I'm meeting with an individual or a group, the foundational structure and procedure is similar. That being said, none of them look exactly the same. Each has developed a unique life of their own based upon the different personalities, focus, timing, location, and other factors involved. Establish a structured format while remaining flexible enough to allow your meetings to grow into exciting times of growth and encouragement.

As you establish a format for your meetings, here are ten questions to ask:

1. *"How often do we want to meet?"* The overall purpose and focus of your meeting times will determine how often you should meet, as will everyone's schedule. Common frequencies are once a month, every other week, or once a week.

2. *"When and where will we meet, and for how long?"* Establish a specific day, time, and location where you will meet, along with the length of your meeting. This will provide a regular time that you can schedule in advance, eventually becoming a natural rhythm in your life.

3. *"Who will send out reminders?"* Identify the person who will send out a regular reminder the day before your meeting, assuring that no one accidentally forgets.

4. *"Under what circumstances will we miss a meeting?"* Commit to each other that you will place a high priority on your meeting times. Do all you can to make sure you attend and respect each other's time by being on time and prepared. If something comes up where you absolutely cannot attend or are going to be late, inform your partner(s) in advance.

5. *"What's our start and end date?"* Establishing an overall start and end date is a great way to implement a natural evaluation point for your meetings and give each other permission to continue on or end your meetings. For example, let's say you decide to start January 1 and go through June 30. Once June 30 rolls around, together you will evaluate whether or not you have achieved your overall purpose and if you want to continue on for another specified period of time or are ready to end your meetings. If you continue meeting, this is also a good time to evaluate how your meetings are going and what (if anything) you can do to improve your time together.

6. *"What will we and won't we talk about?"* Set clear boundaries for what will and won't be discussed during your times together. It is important to make it clear that you will not talk about anyone who is not a part of your meetings, nor will you share personal information about others without their permission. It is also important that you each commit to hold all discussions confidential, unless you agree in advance that it's okay to share something you've discussed. Following these two guidelines will go a long way toward maintaining your integrity and trust with each other.

7. ***"How will we focus our discussions?"*** Find a specific plan that will guide your discussions, give you specific steps to follow to help you achieve your priorities, and help you track your progress. If you are specifically meeting to establish and stay on task in achieving your overall priorities, I recommend you use *The Ultimate Success Formula* and *The Ultimate Success Formula Worksheets* as your discussion guide. If your meetings will be focusing on a specific priority, then find a plan that will be the focus of your meeting times. For recommendations, go to OneShotOneLife.com; you'll find specific plans that we have developed or recommend.

8. ***"What format will we use for our meetings?"*** Effective, productive meetings follow a format to keep everyone focused on what's important. Here's a basic seven-step meeting format to get you started:

    a. **Catch up.** Spend the first few minutes of your meeting catching up on what's going on in each other's lives. Relationships are the most valuable thing in life, so invest time getting to know one other better and sharing life together.

    b. **Review.** Quickly recap what you covered the last time you met, focusing specifically on the progress you reported.

    c. **Share.** Share the progress you've made since your last meeting. Share what you've accomplished, what hasn't work, what you've learned, and what you need to make up or change.

    d. **Learn.** Go over new information you are learning and how you might incorporate it into your plan.

    e. **Process.** Talk about your next steps, ask questions, clarify, and encourage each other to keep moving forward in the process.

f. **Prioritize.** Share what you each want to accomplish with your priorities by the next time you meet. Write down the priorities your success partner will be working on so you can ask about them the next time you meet.

g. **Remind.** Confirm with each other when you will meet next and make any needed changes to your schedule.

9. *"Who will lead our discussions?"* Designate someone who will commit to lead the discussion of your meetings, keeping you focused and on task. This might be the same person, or it might change from meeting to meeting.

10. *"How can we keep things creative and fun?"* Once you have established your regular meetings, it's time to really enjoy them. Once in a while you may want to mix things up and try something new to help you stay razor-sharp, focused, and effective. Here are some ideas my success partners and I have tried successfully:

- Invite a guest speaker to a meeting.
- Hold your meeting in a different location each week.
- Take a field trip to a place that will inspire you toward your priority.
- See a movie that relates to your priority.
- Bring treats and/or beverages.
- Buy a gift for your partner that you know they'd appreciate.
- Encourage each other to share big dreams you want to accomplish one day.
- Randomly write an encouraging note to your partner.
- Celebrate a holiday or birthday together (especially if you're in a group).
- Have a family night where you, your spouses, and your kids get together to hang out and have fun.

A success partner can be a powerful ally as you set out to achieve your priorities and plans. Always remember that having a success partner is a two-way street where everyone involved reaps the benefits of your time together. King Solomon said it best: "Two people are better off than one, for they can help each other succeed. If one person falls, the other can reach out and help. Three are even better, for a triple-braided cord is not easily broken." (Ecclesiastes 4:9–10,12 NLT)

That's why I believe this Multiplier is one of the most remarkably powerful principles you can implement in *The Ultimate Success Formula.*

Now let's take the final steps in filling out *The Ultimate Success Formula Worksheets.*

Multiplier #2: The Remarkable Power Of A Success Partner

___ *Action Step #1*

Go to the worksheets titled "**My Top Priorities.**"

___ *Action Step #2*

If you have chosen to have a success partner(s) for achieving your top priorities, then write in that person's name(s) in the "Success Partner(s)" space on your worksheet.

___ *Action Step #3*

Now go to the "**My Top Priority Plan**" worksheets.

___ *Action Step #4*

If you have chosen to have a success partner(s) for achieving any of your specific plans, write in that person's name(s) in the "Success Partner(s)" space on your worksheet.

Chapter Nine

Be Courageous & Swing Big

I n my office hangs a large poster of Babe Ruth standing before a sold-out crowd of over 62,000 fans at Yankee Stadium during the ceremony to retire his uniform number. Number 3 stands near home plate, holding his hat by his side in one hand and his bat resting on the ground in the other, while the crowd gives him a larger than life standing ovation.

I love his quote printed at the top of the poster: "I swing big, with everything I've got. I hit big, or I miss big. I like to live as big as I can."

And live big he did! During his amazing career, Babe Ruth had 2,174 runs, 2,873 hits, 714 home runs, and 2,213 RBIs.[9] Some amazing numbers! The Great Bambino was undoubtedly one of the greatest baseball players to have ever played the game, even to this day.

I love the constant reminder that when I swing big in life, I will achieve some pretty amazing things along the way! It also pushes me to

---

9 "Career Statistics." BabeRuth.com. http://www.baberuth.com/stats/ (accessed December 11, 2017).

give everything I've got mentally, emotionally, physically, and spiritually to the priorities and plans I set out to achieve.

I want to congratulate you for swinging big by completing *The Ultimate Success Formula* for the first time. I know it's not an easy process, but it is a process that helps people achieve amazing results.

The Ultimate Success Formula is also designed for you to go through on a regular basis. I recommend annually. Each time you go through it you will find the process easier to implement. You will also find yourself more focused on clarifying your priorities and achieving all the things that are important to you.

Trust me, you will swing big and miss big as you set out to achieve your priorities. Don't worry about striking out. The key is to get back up in the batter's box and keep swinging. Swing enough times, and you will start racking up your own runs, hits, home runs, and RBIs. Keep swinging for the fences, my friend.

Also know that you will doubt yourself and wonder whether you should even step onto the field or into the batter's box at all. Don't let doubt and fear keep you from getting in the game. If you don't get in the game, you will miss out on the most incredible moments of your life.

The Gift of Being Courageous

As I shared earlier in this book, my daughter Sydney's passion is dance. She eats, drinks, and sleeps it 24/7. It's a God-given love she's had all her life, and she's been blessed to develop her gift at one of the top dance studios in our city since she was four years old.

Early in 2011, when she was ten years old, Syd was given the honor to perform her first public dance solo at a recital where several hundred people would be in attendance. That's a big deal for a ten-year-old, but she was up to the task. She practiced day in and day out for weeks leading up to the recital.

The night before the recital, during the dress rehearsal, Sydney was given a gift that has helped propel her to become the high-level dancer she is today.

That night, the auditorium was packed with hundreds of dancers along with moms and dads watching the girls' final preparations for the recital the next evening. The closer it came time for Syd and her group to rehearse, the more nervous she became. Minutes before they were to take the stage, Syd ran to Tammie and me sobbing, and as best as we could make out, she was telling us that she didn't want to do it. The more we tried to comfort and assure her that she would do great, the more adamant she became that she was not going to practice or perform her solo.

At that moment, Sydney's dance instructor, the owner of the studio, walked over to her, knelt down in front of her, cradled Syd's face gently in both her hands, and in a tender, confident and assuring tone said, "Sydney, I chose you for this solo because I know you can do it and because you are the best dancer to perform it. You have practiced so hard with your group, and you don't want to let them or yourself down. I know you will be amazing and beautiful. Now I want you to get up on stage and run through it with your group."

Wiping away her tears, holding back new ones, and trying to catch her breath, Sydney slowly made her way to the back of the stage. During the rehearsal Sydney did a great job, considering all that she was emotionally going through. And I'll never forget what she told us on the ride home. "Mom and Dad, tonight was scary," she said. "But now I know I can do a really good job at the recital tomorrow night."

The next night, Sydney performed flawlessly. Good was an understatement! She was amazing and beautiful! As Tammie and I watched, it was our turn to cry, but ours were tears of true joy and gratitude.

After the recital, I told Sydney's instructor, "Thank you so much for giving Sydney **the gift of being courageous** last night. Your intentional encouragement gave her the confidence to not just get on stage, but to also give it her all and absolutely shine."

Sydney Fitzgerald

Sydney's rehearsal night moment with her instructor is what continues to give her the confidence and courage to dream big and swing big as she lives out her passion for dance. She has performed for thousands of people, both in high-level dance groups and solos, with many more to come.

But think about this: What if Sydney hadn't gotten on stage that night of the rehearsal? What if she wouldn't have given it a shot? Would she be where she is today? I highly doubt it. Nor would she be dancing at such a high level today without that key moment in her life.

Don't let fear and doubt keep you from getting up on your stage and performing. Don't let fear and doubt keep you from getting on your field and swinging big. Life is way too short, and the stakes are way too high, to walk away from opportunities that may give you and those around you the greatest benefits of success.

Get up on stage! Step up to the plate! You will be amazing! You will succeed!

Let me close with some encouraging words from King David. In Psalm 37, one of my favorite psalms, he shares some key promises of God that can give us the courage to move full throttle ahead with our priorities.

"Take delight in the Lord, and he will give you your heart's desires. Commit everything you do to the Lord. Trust him, and he will help you . . . Be still in the presence of the Lord, and wait patiently for him to act . . . The Lord directs the steps of the godly. He delights in every detail of their lives. Though they stumble, they will never fall, for the Lord holds them by the hand." (Psalm 37:4–5, 7a, 23–24 NLT)

So once again, congratulations on going through *The Ultimate Success Formula*. I highly recommend you go through *The Ultimate Success Formula* on a regular basis. Most people like to go through it once a year. Over time you may find yourself wanting to go through it every six months or so. Whatever you decide, know that if you make it a regular part of your life, you will be able to look back years from now and celebrate all the incredible things you have accomplished.

And regularly refer to our website at OneShotOneLife.com to check out our latest content and resources specifically designed to help you stop worrying and start winning in the areas of Money, People, Faith, Work, Health, and Sex.

I would also love to hear from you. Feel free to contact me and share what's going on in your life. Go to our website at OneShotOneLife.com and click on the "Contact" tab to send me an email.

Oh, and for the record, this year Tammie and I celebrated our twenty-sixth wedding anniversary! I can honestly say that we are the happiest we have ever been, and I am thankful for the principles in *The Ultimate Success Formula* that helped us get to this point in our relationship.

Remember, you only have One Shot and One Life, so be courageous and swing big every day!

Doug, Tammie, Sydney & Dylan Fitzgerald

Appendix

The Ultimate Success Formula Worksheets

FREE DIGITAL DOWNLOAD

A FREE digital download of **The Ultimate Success Formula Worksheets** is also available at **OneShotOneLife.com/Worksheets**.

IDENTIFYING MY PRIORITIES

MONEY

Needs

❏ _____

❏ _____

❏ _____

❏ _____

❏ _____

Shoulds

❏ _____

❏ _____

❏ _____

❏ _____

❏ _____

Wants

❏ _____

❏ _____

❏ _____

❏ _____

❏ _____

1 = Vital   2 = Important   3 = Can Wait

PEOPLE

Needs

- ❑ _____
- ❑ _____
- ❑ _____
- ❑ _____
- ❑ _____

Shoulds

- ❑ _____
- ❑ _____
- ❑ _____
- ❑ _____
- ❑ _____

Wants

- ❑ _____
- ❑ _____
- ❑ _____
- ❑ _____
- ❑ _____

1 = Vital   2 = Important   3 = Can Wait

IDENTIFYING MY PRIORITIES

FAITH

Needs

- ☐ _____
- ☐ _____
- ☐ _____
- ☐ _____
- ☐ _____

Shoulds

- ☐ _____
- ☐ _____
- ☐ _____
- ☐ _____
- ☐ _____

Wants

- ☐ _____
- ☐ _____
- ☐ _____
- ☐ _____
- ☐ _____

1 = Vital   2 = Important   3 = Can Wait

IDENTIFYING MY PRIORITIES

WORK

Needs

- ❏ _____
- ❏ _____
- ❏ _____
- ❏ _____
- ❏ _____

Shoulds

- ❏ _____
- ❏ _____
- ❏ _____
- ❏ _____
- ❏ _____

Wants

- ❏ _____
- ❏ _____
- ❏ _____
- ❏ _____
- ❏ _____

1 = Vital   2 = Important   3 = Can Wait

IDENTIFYING MY PRIORITIES

HEALTH

Needs

- ☐ _____
- ☐ _____
- ☐ _____
- ☐ _____
- ☐ _____

Shoulds

- ☐ _____
- ☐ _____
- ☐ _____
- ☐ _____
- ☐ _____

Wants

- ☐ _____
- ☐ _____
- ☐ _____
- ☐ _____
- ☐ _____

1 = Vital   2 = Important   3 = Can Wait

IDENTIFYING MY PRIORITIES

OTHER

Needs

- ❑ _____
- ❑ _____
- ❑ _____
- ❑ _____
- ❑ _____

Shoulds

- ❑ _____
- ❑ _____
- ❑ _____
- ❑ _____
- ❑ _____

Wants

- ❑ _____
- ❑ _____
- ❑ _____
- ❑ _____
- ❑ _____

1 = Vital   2 = Important   3 = Can Wait

MY TOP PRIORITIES

Money

1. _____

   My Why: _____

2. _____

   My Why: _____

People

1. _____

   My Why: _____

2. _____

   My Why: _____

Faith

1. _____

   My Why: _____

2. _____

   My Why: _____

Work

1. _____

   My Why: _____

2. _____

   My Why: _____

MY TOP PRIORITIES

Health

1. _____

   My Why: _____

2. _____

   My Why: _____

Other

1. _____

   My Why: _____

2. _____

   My Why: _____

Evaluation Dates/Times: _____

Success Partner(s): _____

MY TOP PRIORITY PLAN

MONEY

Priority

_____

_____

My Why

_____

_____

Proven Plan

_____

_____

Start Date: _____ Completion Date: _____

Weekly Schedule: _____

Evaluation Dates/Times: _____

Success Partner(s): _____

To-Do List / Notes

❑ _____

❑ _____

❑ _____

❑ _____

❑ _____

MY TOP PRIORITY PLAN

PEOPLE

Priority

_____

_____

My Why

_____

_____

Proven Plan

_____

_____

Start Date: _____ Completion Date: _____

Weekly Schedule: _____

Evaluation Dates/Times: _____

Success Partner(s): _____

To-Do List / Notes

❑ _____

❑ _____

❑ _____

❑ _____

❑ _____

MY TOP PRIORITY PLAN

FAITH

Priority

_____

_____

My Why

_____

_____

Proven Plan

_____

_____

Start Date: _____ Completion Date: _____

Weekly Schedule: _____

Evaluation Dates/Times: _____

Success Partner(s): _____

To-Do List / Notes

- ❑ _____
- ❑ _____
- ❑ _____
- ❑ _____
- ❑ _____

MY TOP PRIORITY PLAN

WORK

Priority

_____

_____

My Why

_____

_____

Proven Plan

_____

_____

Start Date: _____ Completion Date: _____

Weekly Schedule: _____

Evaluation Dates/Times: _____

Success Partner(s): _____

To-Do List / Notes

❑ _____

❑ _____

❑ _____

❑ _____

❑ _____

HEALTH

Priority

_____

_____

My Why

_____

_____

Proven Plan

_____

_____

Start Date: _____ Completion Date: _____

Weekly Schedule: _____

Evaluation Dates/Times: _____

Success Partner(s): _____

To-Do List / Notes

❏ _____

❏ _____

❏ _____

❏ _____

❏ _____

MY TOP PRIORITY PLAN

OTHER

Priority

_____

_____

My Why

_____

_____

Proven Plan

_____

_____

Start Date: _____ Completion Date: _____

Weekly Schedule: _____

Evaluation Dates/Times: _____

Success Partner(s): _____

To-Do List / Notes

❑ _____

❑ _____

❑ _____

❑ _____

❑ _____

About the Author

 Doug Fitzgerald is a motivational and life-changing speaker, personal coach and author. Known for his authentic and relational approach to life, Doug's real, honest, and transparent communication are admired for being focused on helping others achieve their life priorities.

Doug started his career as a radio disc jockey for 7 years (hosting a #1 Top 40 Morning Show) and served as a Youth & Executive Pastor for 13 years before turning his attention to starting and building a multi-million-dollar business over the past 11 years.

Doug currently resides in Nebraska and has been married to his wife Tammie for over 26 years. They have two children, Dylan and Sydney.

To have him share his motivational message, speak, or bring *The Ultimate Success Formula Seminar* to your business, group, or organization, you can contact him through his website at OneShotOneLife.com.

Social media information:
Facebook: dougfitzgerald
Twitter: Doug_Fitzgerald
Instagram: dougfitzgerald
YouTube: dougfitzgerald

About ONESHOT. ONELIFE.®

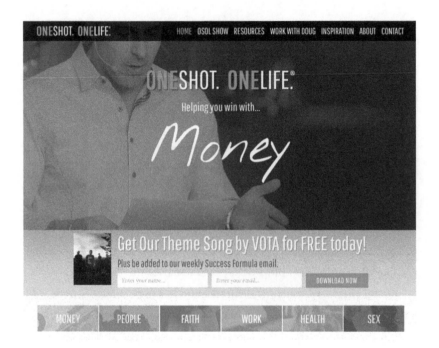

There's a great proverb that says that when you search for wisdom and then use common sense and discernment to apply it, then you will be able to stop worrying and start winning. And that's our goal at **ONE**SHOT. **ONE**LIFE. At **OneShotOneLife.com** we provide tools and resources to help people stop worrying and start winning in the areas of Money, People, Faith, Work, Health and Sex.

Go to **OneShotOneLife.com** to learn more about our:

- FREE Weekly "Success Formula" Email
- FREE Downloads, Including The **ONE**SHOT. **ONE**LIFE. Theme Song
- The **ONE**SHOT. **ONE**LIFE. Show (OSOL Show)
- Online Course
- Seminars
- Live Events
- Mastermind Groups
- One-On-One Coaching
- And More

Morgan James
Speakers Group

www.TheMorganJamesSpeakersGroup.com

We connect Morgan James published
authors with live and online events
and audiences who will benefit
from their expertise.

CPSIA information can be obtained
at www.ICGtesting.com
Printed in the USA
LVHW01s1329260518
578458LV00001B/1/P